HER VISION

HER VISION

USING THE D.I.V.A. FRAMEWORK
FOR AN INSPIRED LIFE AND BUSINESS

FALESHA RAQUEL

Copyright © 2020 Falesha Raquel

All rights reserved. No part of this book may be reproduced, stored, or transmitted by any means—whether auditory, graphic, mechanical, or electronic—without written permission of both publisher and author, except in the case of brief excerpts used in critical articles and reviews. Unauthorized reproduction of any part of this work is illegal and is punishable by law.

Published by Falesha Raquel

ISBN: 978-1-9991456-0-6 Paperback
ISBN: 978-1-9991456-1-3 eBook

CONTENTS

Part One

MY STORY

This book is dedicated to the entire Mangallon family, especially to my younger cousins who look up to me. Romere, Mykaela, Jaylene, Melia and Ayanna—know that you can achieve anything in life as long as you have the right mindset. My siblings who I love so much—Aaron, Gary, Gemel, Givani, Joshua, and Renèe.

My hardworking mother, Jocelyn.

My father, Gary.

My amazing husband, Shane, you're my world.

My awesome assistant, Heather, I don't know how I'd do it without you.

And to all the dancers out there, never stop dancing.

I love you!

~ Falesha Raquel

The material in this book is the truth, as I know it, as I experienced it through my eyes. I know that each of us has our own perception of the truth. I recognize that other people's memories of the events may be different than my own. The book was not intended to harm anyone, hurt anyone's feelings, or portray them negatively. Everyone involved in the publication, marketing, and support of this book all confirm there is no intention of harm, hurt, or disparagement.

I have changed names, made tweaks to settings and descriptions, to allow people to remain anonymous. To the best of my ability, I have remained honest to my perception of the truth.

INTRODUCTION

As someone in the creative industry, you might be feeling uncertain. You may be indecisive about what choices to make in order to show your art to the world. You know you have a talent, and you want to give the world a better view of it. But you might feel stuck—like you don't know how to get there.

You probably have a few people around you who also believe in you and say things like, "You're so talented," or, "You should really go for this; you're so good." While inspiring, hearing those kinds of things can also cause anxiety if you don't know where to start, what to do next, where to go or who to talk to. You might be yearning for the next level but not know where that next level is. You may be scared to take the leap and really put your all into your art for fear that it might either turn into work that you stop enjoying, or for fear that it might not work out.

I totally get it. I've lived it. And I want to share with you the ups and downs and ins and outs of starting a business centered around your art. I can tell you that it's not easy, but if you were born to be a singer, a dancer, a painter, an actor, a comedian, or a performer of any kind, I may as well say it straight right from the get-go: That pull in your heart will continue to pull you until you give it your best shot.

Easier said than done, right?

For sure. And this is exactly why I wrote this book.

Learning how to make something of your passion and talent in this world is something that you can really only achieve by jumping in and taking action, then learning from each mistake or win and growing along the way. There's no universal theory or method to it—you learn how to run a business focused around your talent by actually *doing* it. That being said, it is helpful to hear about others' experiences who have done the same thing or something similar. I wrote this book to share with you all of the disappointments and hard lessons I had to learn—the hard way, no less—and what I needed to do in order to keep going. I sure didn't do it alone. I had mentorship, counsel, and support along the way. I studied other artists and learned about how they built careers around their art. Now I want to be a voice of support and motivation for you.

I have heard so many talented people I know say, "I only spend time in the studio on the weekend. It's more of a hobby, really. The rest of the week I have to pay the bills." If you're working a corporate job to pay the bills and practicing your art after hours, that's fine—if your art really is a hobby, and you're truly fulfilled in your main work. The trouble is, this isn't the case for many artists. Too often, I hear that people hate their weekday jobs, or they hate having to stay up all hours of the night working in the hospitality industry just to do their best to make ends meet. In the narrow cracks between the hours of their work schedule, errands, and social life, they struggle to find time to do what they really love.

Let's face it: The expression "starving artist" didn't come out of nowhere. In the past, it has been difficult for artists to find enough work to make their art a full-time job. But why is that? Is it because there aren't enough booking or hiring opportunities? Is it because the general public doesn't care for art? Is it because people don't like live music, or dance performances, or beautiful artistic creations? Is it because there's too much competition and not enough demand? No—it's none of those things. If an artist isn't making money, it's because (1) they don't know how to package their art as a sellable product, and (2) they don't know how to run their art as a business. This is what I want to help you with.

I started my dance company when I was sixteen years old. I had no idea what I was doing. I just knew I needed to dance every day, that I had to open it, and that I would figure it out. Many years and challenging lessons later, I did. I made the decision that I wanted to be able to live a good, comfortable life making money doing what I loved. *Diva Diverse* is now an international dance company, based out of two major cities in North America, Miami and Toronto, and runs an average of 1000 dance performances a year.

I also got married in my early twenties and began a life-long partnership with my amazing husband. There were many times I felt overwhelmed, and there were many roles I had to fulfill that I didn't know right away how to fulfill. I had to build the ship as it was sailing. I learned what I had to do as a businesswoman, an artist, and a wife, to create a life I loved.

I did not have an easy time getting to where I am now. There were many ups and downs, and, truth be told, many times that I didn't know how I was going to persevere. I had tough times where money was extremely tight and I felt defeated. I experienced extreme highs while I was performing with my company and watching the company grow and grow, only to fall to the extreme low of realizing that I had been taken advantage of by people I had trusted and losing a ton of money, setting me far back again.

There were many times I wanted to give up. I was in a court battle for two years. I lost hundreds of thousands of dollars in a scam. I had trouble in my marriage a few years in, and most recently, have had trouble getting pregnant. So no, not everything has been perfect. People look at me and they see the successful me. I portray that image, and it gives the impression that it was always easy for me. I am going to show you in this book what is *behind* the glamour, the hair and makeup.

As you'll read about, I resorted to getting a "full-time, secure and stable" job in a bank at one point when things were really difficult financially for me. Money was so tight at that time that getting a stable job seemed a way better option than worrying about how I was going to pay my bills anymore. But I quickly learned that it wasn't the right path for me. Going to a job every day that I didn't care for, and not being able to dance every day, started to suffocate me very fast. I knew then that, no matter what, I had to find a way to succeed as an artist in business. I had to dance, and I had to make a stable living doing it.

Thomas Edison tried a hundred times before he invented the light bulb. Success takes time and the willingness to fail over and over, as well as the willingness to learn and grow. But I did it, and you can too.

The first part of the book is my story. I share these stories with you so that when or if you come across some of the same things in your own journey, you can say to yourself, *Oh—I remember Falesha went through something like this. Let me go back to that chapter and see what happened with that situation in her life. How did she handle it?* Use my stories as much as you can to help you on your own path.

I share some of the most scared moments in my life in this book. I also share some of the happiest moments, some of the most depressing ones, and even some of the most embarrassing ones. I laugh about the embarrassing ones today, but these are moments I was so embarrassed at the time to want to share with anyone that it took me until now—several years later—to actually have the courage to talk about them! People asked me while I was writing this book, "Aren't you uncomfortable sharing your life story with so many people?" Yes, of course, I am uncomfortable with having my life be so public. It is much more comfortable to keep everything inside and to myself. But I truly believe that the things that happened in my life didn't happen for just me—I believe they happened to me so that I can help others—and maybe you—through similar situations.

My hope is that through reading my story, you will be inspired to take action, and that you will see that you can make a business of your art, too. You may still be in university, or you may be just opening a business, or you may be afraid to start. Wherever you are at in your own story, I hope you can find something of value in mine.

In the second part of the book, I share with you the five things that helped me the most on my journey. As you'll discover when you read *Chapter 1*, I had an experience not too long ago that I will never forget. Up until that point, I was living my life with a particular understanding and view of things, and I had done fairly well with that view, and that moment forever changed me. I realized my difficult circumstances and the lessons I'd learned translated into four things that would help me run a better business and be a better artist: (1) Determination, (2) Intelligence, (3) Value, and (4) Attitude. Knowing now how central to my success these four things have been, and continue to be, in business as an artist, I look forward to sharing them with you so you can apply them in your own unique way in your life and business.

I wrote in a diary my entire life, and it was one of the ways I organized my thoughts and got clear on what I wanted. As you'll read about in Chapter 9, I wrote about my husband before I met him. I wrote about my business along the way. I wrote about what I was learning, and it helped me process the lessons I was learning. I always say artists need to write. *You need to write.*

There are a few additional things I want to mention before we begin. First of all, you do not have to naturally be prone to running a business in order to be successful at doing so. As human beings, we are naturally hard on ourselves. We can have a tendency to read about someone else's success and automatically think it's not possible for us. I assure you: None of the journey I'm about to take you on was easy for me at the time. None of it! Every day there were new challenges coming to the surface and new fears arising in my mind that made my life feel like an obstacle course. All of the things you say to yourself about yourself, your art, and the possibility of turning your art into a business, I probably said to myself at one point. Heck, I still have fears and doubts—they never fully go away. But fears and doubts are bad predictors of success. You can have both at the same time. I invite you to notice when your fears and doubts come up as you read, to jot them down in the space provided or in a journal, and to simultaneously look for ways success can be true for you.

The second point I want to mention is that when you read and start applying what's in this book, it's not going to create quick, overnight, automatic success. Success is a process, and a non-linear one at that. There's going to be good stuff and bad stuff. I'm not promising all the finer things in life; I'm inviting you to open up this chapter in your life and really go for it.

Third, this is a book where art meets business told through the lens of my experience. This isn't a business *how-to*—I am not an MBA professor, or a business or economics teacher. It is a portrait of my life, and a summary of lessons that I hope can help you through some of your own challenges.

Fourth, there are going to be some things that you have to learn yourself. Not everyone's path is the same, and your tests and challenges might not look exactly like mine. A huge challenge for me might not occur as a huge challenge for you, and vice versa. This book will not provide a solution for everything that comes up for you. Use it rather as an example that you can come back to, to remind yourself that having faith can get you through *anything*. The actual exact events of my story are less important than the fact that I got through them.

Finally, I want to encourage you to read this book as *real life*. As you're reading my story, I invite you to think of *yourself* in each moment. You may be reading what I decided and did in those moments, but imagine yourself in your own life as you're reading. Let my story be a map that provides some direction, and use the map while you're in your own car, on your own road.

The world needs your art. You can make something of your talents. Your art can support you. Your talents were given to you so that you would have everything you need for a great life. I am so grateful that you are coming along on this journey with me. Let's begin.

PART ONE

My Story

Chapter 1

AN UNFORGETTABLE EXPERIENCE

*There is no greater gift you can give or receive than to honor your
calling. It's why you were born. And how you become most truly alive.*

-OPRAH WINFREY

It was a Friday night in January, 2016. I was exhausted from my belly dance shows, so I got off stage from my last performance that night and headed home.

I was exhausted from the day, but I was also drained from two years of personal and professional turmoil and setback after setback in the business. I had been dancing on autopilot for a while. I was distracted, going through the motions. I hadn't had a break in months. Money was tight. There was no such thing as a break.

On stage, dancing, you'd have no idea I was going through a rough patch in the business. Even on autopilot, I would always bring energy to the stage. With every booking, I would show up and go out on that floor and give the audience my all. No one would be able to tell I was going through anything.

But when I'd get off stage, it would hit me.

And that night was no different. I got home, exhausted, ready to rest for the night.

Walking into the kitchen, I realized that my husband, Shane, had a couple of friends over. They were in the living room watching television. I noticed a plastic container full of what looked like brownies on the table.

Shane came into the kitchen to give me a kiss hello.

I'd often regret that during this particular phase of the business, I didn't have much energy left for my husband by the time I'd get home. It weighed even heavier on me. "Babe, I'm so tired . . . I'm sweaty."

There was glitter everywhere. My makeup was a mess. My hair was flat and as tired as my body. He kissed me anyway. I married a good man.

"Thanks, Babe. Love you too." My curiosity got the best of me then. "Oh, by the way, what's that on the table?"

One of Shane's friends, Kareem, came into the kitchen and answered me eagerly. "Brownies."

I assumed it was an offer. "Oh, awesome. I like brownies. Thanks!" Who would say no to that?

"No—they're a different kind of brownies. They have weed in them."

"What? Really?" I'm pretty sure my eyes opened a little wider because Shane and Kareem both chuckled at my reaction. "I've heard about these. Can I try one?"

Shane stepped in pretty quickly. "But Babe, you don't even smoke."

"Well, I've tried it before. I hate being high but I've never tried these." Shane looks out for me, but he won't stop me from doing something I really want to do if he doesn't think it's going to hurt me. He imagined a small piece would be harmless. So did I. By that point, the anticipation in the air was thick. "I guess I'll just try it."

I remember looking at the brownie and thinking, *I know better. I shouldn't do this because if I do this, I'm vulnerable.* At the same time, I was tired of being the good girl all the time. I looked at the guys and thought if they could hang out and be carefree like that, I could do. I knew I needed to relax, and I thought it might be the best way to do it. I just needed a break.

I legit took a *quarter*. Like a tiny *fraction* of one of them. I just wanted a little taste.

Nothing happened. It wasn't that interesting. I decided to get into the shower and change. "You guys have fun."

After my shower, I went back to the kitchen, cut a slice of apple pie, and warmed it up. After putting ice cream on top, I went upstairs to the bedroom to eat it. I didn't want Shane and his friends to see me eating apple pie and ice cream that late and either make fun of me or want a piece of it themselves. I didn't want to share it with them. You know guys, how they just devour everything. And besides, this was my little moment of peace. Just me, myself, and this apple pie with ice cream.

So back up to the bedroom I went, wrapped in my towel, with my feet hanging off the end of the bed. I sat, eating my apple pie and ice cream, and it was so good.

From the tip of my toe to the top of my head, I felt a little tingling feeling come over me. I suddenly realized I was high. I finished the pie and threw on a little pajama dress so I could be appropriate because the guys were still downstairs. I put my dish in the sink and went into the living room. "Hey, guys."

They were playing a basketball video game and barely noticed me. "Hey," one of them said, glued to the screen.

"Sorry to interrupt—are you guys high?"

Kareem mumbled, "We feel nice; we're good."

"You're good?"

"Yeah, we're good."

Shane looked at me. "You okay, Babe?"

"I'm high! I'm so high, guys!" I couldn't believe how weird I felt, from the tip of my toe to the top of my head. I started going on and on about what was happening and they took turns looking at me as if to say, *What is wrong with you?* "I'm floating . . . I feel so weird . . . how do you guys feel? Do you feel tingly at all? Tell me how you feel . . . tell me exactly what's happening to you right now."

"Falesha! You're totally tripping!"

It seemed obvious. "Well, yeah! What do I do?" I felt so high and overwhelmed. I sat down in the kitchen and started to see images of my life flash before me. "Woah . . . why am I seeing my whole life?"

Shane came in. "What do you mean?"

"Ok . . . this is different now. I'm not high anymore."

"Babe, there's no way. You're still high. Just chill here for a bit. I'll get you some water. Try to relax."

"No, you don't understand, Babe . . . seriously. I'm not high anymore. But I'm seeing my whole life. I don't know what's going on." Time from that moment was counting down. I was seeing visions, as if I was in a dream, but I was awake.

Shane was trying to snap me out of it. "Shake it off. Come on, have some water." He handed me a full glass.

"No—I can't shake it. There's nothing I can do." I saw my wedding day, and everything that happened at my wedding, and then I was a teenager, then a child back when my grandparents were alive, and then I was a baby. I saw the three cats on my grandmother's sweater when she was holding me. "Okay—I'm legit seeing my life flash before my eyes! This is what you see when you die!" I started to panic.

"Babe, no. You're fine. You're just high. Shake it off. Seriously. You're starting to freak me out." Worried by this point, he told his friends to leave.

They left, and we went into the bathroom and Shane had me splash water on my face to try to break the high. I just kept saying, "Hon, I'm not high. You have to understand. I'm telling you that something's going to happen. I think I'm going to die because I'm seeing everything flash. But I think my body is disconnected from what's happening. I'm disconnected somehow. I'm not in the same reality."

He helped me onto the bed and when the visions got down to me as a baby, I started passing out. I was laying on Shane's lap, and then I was a fetus. I had the feeling of being warm and being inside my mom's womb. I could feel a heartbeat.

I woke up and gasped for air.

Shane jumped. "Are you okay?"

I thought I was given another chance or something. I was pretty freaked out.

Then I saw a red female figure standing beside the bed close to me. Without her saying anything, I already knew what she was going to do. She was going to go into my body and possess me because I was vulnerable—my soul had left because I was high. "Shane, you need to lock me in my walk-in closet and just leave me there for a little bit." I didn't tell him what I saw at the time. I thought she was going to make me do something to harm him. And it started to become so real to me, that sometimes when people do terrible things, they're under the influence of an evil spirit that's attacked them.

Even in my vulnerable state, I kept saying in my mind, *NO! You can't attack me. There's no way you're going to enter my body and make me harm anyone.*

Then out of nowhere—I don't even know how I knew to ask for this—I said, "Archangel Michael, Archangel Gabriel, my guardian angel . . . I need you here with me right now. Wherever you are, do you see this thing? Are you seeing what's in front of me?" I was talking to them, and no one was responding. "Where is everyone? Hello? Can anyone hear me?"

I don't know if she got scared, but she ended up leaving. I started shaking and sweating.

"Why are you shaking?"

"I think you need to take me to the hospital."

"No, we're not going to the hospital. You're going to be fine."

I soaked the whole bed with my sweat. I finally calmed down because the red female figure was gone. I closed my eyes, tired from fighting it. I fell asleep, but I wasn't fully sleeping.

I found myself up in space, with a divine presence. The only way I can describe it is that I was in some kind of meeting to set me straight. I started talking first: "God, please put me back in my body! I'm so tired. What's happening? Why am I here?"

No response.

I saw my guardian angel and he said, "We told her, but she doesn't want to listen."

Silence.

The divine presence finally spoke in a deep, full voice that I can't even describe. "Falesha, you know better. You know your purpose. You know you shouldn't have done that."

And I was like, "I know! I know!" I was talking to him like he was Dad. As if I was begging, saying, "Please don't ground me! I do know better, but I was just so stressed out." I kept going on and on.

Silence.

When you're under the influence, I believe you open up your spirit a little bit and enable other things to take you over. My grandparents were religious, and I somehow always knew that growing up as a child. I must have learned it from them. I realized in that moment I had allowed that to happen.

"You know better."

"I know I know better. I don't know what I was thinking. I'm so stupid; I shouldn't have done that."

"But you know. You know you're not supposed to do those things."

For anyone who knew me from when I was a kid, this must sound crazy coming from someone like me. I was never such a spiritual person. I didn't even understand what "spiritual" meant, even though I believed in God.

Finally, I said, "Please, I'll do anything. Shane doesn't have kids yet. I promise to give him kids. I'll be a great mom. How about my business? How about all of my goals? I have so many goals and so much to do still. I can't stay here; I need to go back! You have to give me another chance! You can't just let me stay here. I've worked so hard on earth!"

"Falesha, we have to go over this." He was so calm about telling me about what I had done wrong.

"I promise I will stay on track; I will do my life's purpose. I know what it is. I'm not going to waste my life on distractions."

He didn't say anything else; he was just giving me a warm feeling like the sun.

I felt like I was up there with him for months. It felt way longer than just the overnight that I slept.

When I woke up the next morning, my husband was still beside me. He hadn't gone to work because he was worried about me.

He thought I'd had an anxiety attack. I have had anxiety before, and this was not anxiety. It was real. I literally saw my life flash before my eyes. It's how I know I was at my boiling point.

I felt like I had been reborn. Even though my body was an adult, it was like my soul was a kid again. I started remembering things, and I knew I was meant to serve the purpose that I was originally given.

If we don't live our purpose and we got off track, we will be reminded. I know that now, 100 percent.

There were many years before that night in January 2016 that I was distracted. After my meeting with my maker, everything changed. I got back in the driver's seat after that.

My perception of life also changed so much. I see now how important it is to drop my pride and ego to understand my life. I'm in the entertainment industry, and I understand we have to do things to market ourselves in order to get to work in our field. Fine—but there's a time to take off the mask and be a real person.

There were so many signs before that moment that I should have pulled my socks up. I was going through so much. There was a point leading up to that meeting where things had changed for the worse in my life. I had a friend sit me down once after a lot of my long, curly hair had broken off after I had dyed it bleach blonde. She sat me down and pulled up some pictures of me. "Look at these pictures. Look at how healthy you were here." Then she pointed to a few pictures from just before that fateful night. "Now look at these. What's going on with you now? Do you see the difference?"

I really did. I could clearly see the change.

Looking back now, I can see I needed a divine presence to intervene at that point in my life.

So where did I go wrong? What led me to that point where I needed to be refocused? What was I doing right, and more importantly, what did I need to change?

I invite you on my journey.

Chapter 2

CHILDHOOD

I've found that growing up means being honest. About
what I want. What I need. What I feel. Who I am.
-LIVELIFEHAPPY

I was born in 1987. My mom was seventeen years old when she had me; I was premature weighing four pounds, born at thirty-one weeks. I was mostly raised by my grandparents during my early years. We spoke Tagalog, and our household was primarily Filipino, a different language than any of my friends at school. I would bring different food than my friends brought to school. I'd open up my lunch bag and they'd say, "What is that?" with a weird look on their faces.

I'd say, "Oh—it's . . . you wouldn't understand."

They'd have something like the "Lunchables" packages with crackers and little pieces of cheese, and I thought that was so cool. And here my grandparents were packing me actual home-cooked meals made of our kind of food! I was jealous about it, but they didn't have the kind of money to buy me a five-dollar lunch meal every day. When I look back now, I can see that the food that my grandparents made me was way better than any processed meal. The food they made me was rice and chicken with soup and vegetables on the side, similar to pho, which is quite popular these days—I got a real meal every day that I would pay fifteen dollars for now as a grown woman. But when I was a kid, it made me feel like I was the odd one out. I spent a lot of time when I was young realizing I didn't fit in with my classmates.

I discovered young that I needed to be in entertainment. I needed an outlet to express myself. I loved the attention. My very first performance was my aunt and uncle's wedding day. I was seven years old.

I was very close with my aunt and uncle. They didn't have kids yet, so they loved bringing me to MarineLand and African Lion Safari. My father wasn't in the picture when I was growing up, and my mom was finishing up school and starting her career path, so having my aunt and uncle and my grandma and grandpa around so much was really important to me. It gave me the comfort of knowing I had two people to focus on for the moments we were together. So when my aunt and uncle told me they were getting married, I was happy for them but worried at the same time. Who was going to take me to the parks and the zoo now? I was worried about what was going to happen when they had their own kids. I didn't want to be forgotten.

When they told me I was going to be the solo dancer on their wedding day, I lost it (in a good way!) "Wow—what do you mean? You mean I'm going to perform in front of all 400 people? Their wedding was going to be huge.

They said yes and told me that, on top of that, they were going to include my cousins—two on each side of me—and that I could do the choreography because I was the dancer.

I couldn't wait. Little seven-year-old FeFe was out-of-my-tree excited. "Guys, I've got this. Give me the song." It was Colin Lucas' Dollar Wine. You know the one: "Cent . . . five cent . . . ten cent . . . dollar." They wanted it to be a Caribbean theme.

They must have given me a year to prepare for it, or at least that's what it felt like to me at the time. I wanted to make them really proud. I wanted them to remember it forever.

From that point onward, literally every Sunday, I rounded all of us up in the basement at one of my cousin's houses. There were three of us girls and two boys. My mom had previously put me in a few ballet, jazz, and tap dance classes whenever we could afford it, but other than that the five of us had no prior dance experience. I gave them pep talks every week. "Guys, we've got to be serious about this. We're never going to have this wedding day again. This is only going to happen once, and it's going to be on video for the rest of our lives." It was all I could think about.

My cousins were not dancers. They were pretty stressed out. Over and over you could hear my voice fill the basement. "Let's go! Five, six, seven, eight! You've got to take that down lower. Make bigger circles." They must have felt like I was putting them through boot camp!

To me, I was hired for a big job. We were responsible for putting on a show. I wanted us to look professional so I put us all in matching outfits of white shirts and black pants.

The day of the wedding, we needed to be crisp, so I told them to make sure their shirts were ironed and, of course, to make sure they had their shoes.

I remember when I walked into the hall, I was shocked to see what a chandelier looks like in person. There were so many diamonds! I had never seen anything like it before. We didn't have lavish things like chandeliers at home. We had regular lights. We didn't spend money on pretty things. We spent money on things we needed, like groceries. I felt like a princess at a ball.

The show went off without a hitch. I remember looking at the 400 of my aunt and uncle's friends and our family on their feet clapping when the music stopped and being so happy they liked it. The response was over-whelmingly positive. I was in love. I said to myself, *How do I do this forever?*

They even gave us money! Filipinos have a tradition where they pin money on the bride and groom on your wedding day, but we did so well they actually pinned forty dollars on me. It felt like a million dollars. I felt rich in that moment and it was all because of dancing.

~~~
~~~

Before all of this happened, a situation unfolded behind the scenes that I rarely talk about. In fact, most people don't know this about me. When people look at me, today, they often think my life is perfect. They think I have a perfect house, a perfect marriage, perfect dogs . . . but I did not grow up having the perfect childhood. There were many years I didn't know what to do about a situation at home. I didn't know how to get through it or where to go for help.

I'm telling this part of my story, not because I want to expose the dark behavior of people I grew up with, but because I know so many women go through something like this and they go through it alone, not talking to anyone about it and feeling like it's their fault that it's happening.

My friends always had "more" than I did growing up, and they all had father figures in their lives. My mom was a single mom, and she struggled. Bless her heart, she tried so hard but always ended up in and out of bad relationships. I lived with my grandparents until I was in the third grade. I moved in with my mom at that point because she was now able to take care of me. I remember her saying, "I'm responsible now, and I want to do my best being a mother to Falesha. I want you to allow me to be with my daughter." It caused a big fight between her and my grandparents, but eventually, I moved in with my mom.

Living with my mom was so different from living with my grandparents. My mom lived on her own, but she had a boyfriend at home all the time. My grandparents had a strong, loving marriage. I went from a household where I was immersed in my culture and our Filipino ways to being with my mom and her boyfriend who did not practice the ways of our culture at all. I absolutely love our culture so much. I think people are so blessed to have cultural roots and traditions that they practice together as a family, regardless of what the culture is. I think culture is beautiful, and I immediately missed it.

We really didn't have much at all. My mom was also supporting her boyfriend, and it often felt like a full house. I also wasn't a fan of the way my mom's boyfriend treated her. I remember saying to my mom one day, "When I grow up, I will never, ever marry a guy like him!" She was often upset. I never saw anything like that with my grandparents, so I knew it didn't have to be that way.

I didn't get along very well with my mom's boyfriend. When I would leave for school in the morning, he would be sitting on the couch, watching sports. When I would come home from school, he would still be in the same position, sitting on the couch, watching sports. I would say to my mom, "Mom, why doesn't he have a job? Why doesn't he do anything?"

One day I needed help with my homework. I asked him to help me spell the word "window." I wasn't sure at the time if it had a "w" at the end or not. What happened next surprised me: He couldn't help me spell it. I said to my mom that night, "Mom, he doesn't know how to spell the word 'window.'" She helped me spell it and quickly changed the subject.

I came to accept that my mom had chosen this person to be her partner and went on with my life. Things took a turn for the worse at home when I was in the eighth and ninth grade. My mom's boyfriend started to reveal himself to me sexually. He would wait until I was alone and get undressed in front of me.

I remember telling my cousin first. I said, "Hey, you know Kevin? He walks around naked in front of me all the time. Does he do that to you?" It was so strange to me, and I wanted to find out if it was something he did to everyone, or if he only did it to me. I remember being really grossed out. I used to cry about it a lot. They were worried about him potentially raping me. We told my older cousin about it and she said, "Yeah, he does that to me too when I babysit you guys."

It felt like it lasted *forever*. It was the hardest time in my life. Having to go home and have dinner with a pedophile, and sit with my brother and my mom and act like everything was normal . . . it was awful. I was always trying to get out of the house before my mom and brother did. I started to try to make my own routine. I would try to leave early in the mornings. I would try to stay at dance rehearsals extra late after school. If I knew my mom was going to be home at 8:00 p.m., I'd get home at 8:15 p.m. I would stay out as much as I could.

We lived in an apartment, so I would play in the hallway and hang out with my church friends. I started going to church with a friend to get out of the house on weekends. I'd go to church on Saturdays for the whole day and sing in the choir on Sundays. I even did a Wednesday Bible study just to get away from him. If I had to stay home and do my homework, I would literally lock myself in my bedroom because I did not want to see him at all.

I would do the best I could to stand up for myself. I used to tell him he was disgusting and ask him why he didn't go get a job and do something with his life. I used to call him out on it. "Why are you doing this? Why are you touching yourself? Can you just stop already?" I was as strong as I could be with him, but I was terrified to tell my mom about it.

I learned there's a difference between being strong and being smart. He was my stepdad. I used to have so much fun with him. We'd go fishing, we'd go bike riding on trails . . . I had a good relationship with him. He was supposed to be my father figure. But I also wasn't naïve. I knew right from wrong. I'd say, "Stop doing this. You're Mom's boyfriend; I'm Mom's daughter. You're an adult; I'm a kid." I was pretty transparent. I didn't hold anything back. I wasn't scared of him, but I was scared to tell my mom because I wasn't sure what the outcome would be.

It took a lot of courage, but finally I was able to tell her. I remember going back and forth between my cousins that day saying, "Today's the day, guys. I'm going to tell her today. I'm telling my mom what he does." But I remember the fear. I didn't want to hurt her. I had seen her try so hard for so long to have her relationship work, and it wasn't working.

Knowing my younger brother was out at a friend's house that evening, I decided to take the leap. I always protected my brother by not exposing him to the negativity that surrounded our family from time to time. This is definitely something I never made him privy to.

I went into her room, and they were lying on her bed watching an episode of *The Young and the Restless* together. I said, "Hey, can I talk to you for a moment, Mom?" I was so nervous.

I turned the TV off. "Mom, there's something I have to tell you about Kevin." I looked right at him, and I could tell he was worried about what

I was going to say. I said, "Mom, it's been a long time, but he shows his body parts to me and does stuff in front of me."

She said, "Excuse me, what?"

"Yeah mom . . . he tells me to come to him, and he shows his body parts to me . . . and I don't think it's right. It's just not appropriate."

She didn't seem to believe me. "That's crazy talk. Are you sure it's not just in your head? He would never do anything to hurt you. He's your stepdad."

"What do you mean he wouldn't do anything to hurt me? He hasn't done anything to hurt me because I won't let him. But he shows his body parts to me, and he plays with himself in front of me. And one time, Mom, I took a spatula and I threw it at his head before leaving for school."

"You did what?"

"Yeah. Remember that time he had a scratch on his head and he was bleeding? And he said that he got it from shaving?"

"Yeah . . ."

"That was because I threw a spatula at his head. I threw it at him because he told me to touch him. He threw the spatula back at me, and then I took off for school and had to bear that the entire day. I even told my cousin Lisa. I'm telling you the truth."

She sounded very businesslike. Uninterested. "And how long has this been going on for?"

"Two years."

She turned to Kevin. "Did you do that to my daughter?"

"Why would I do that to your daughter? I'm her stepdad. She's making it up. She must be practicing her acting skills."

"Well, I don't understand why she would say something like that then." They barely took their eyes off the television. When I think back, I'm sure it was out of shame on his part and disbelief on my mom's part.

Either way, I perceived it as she didn't believe me. They didn't talk about it again after that. Well at least not in front of me. She stayed with him.

Years later, she found him cheating with another woman.

I found out later my aunt slapped him in the face for coming on to her at a laundromat one day, and my two cousins came forward as well.

She finally ended up divorcing him, and he's now history.

I learned at that young age that I couldn't control anyone else's behavior; all I could do was control my own. I couldn't control what Kevin did, but I could tell him it was wrong and not participate or fall into some sort of trap. I couldn't control whether or not my mom believed me, but I could control whether or not I told her and continued to let her know that it was absolutely true. At some point, I think I accepted that. I learned from the situation. I think I identified my boundaries early—what was okay with me and what wasn't—and I stuck to them.

It breaks my heart that this kind of thing happens to so many women and they don't come forward about it. And sometimes when they do, people don't believe them. So many people are going through this alone. Know that you're not alone.

~~~

After the performance at my aunt and uncle's wedding, I did more and more dancing with my family and friends. Everyone knew I was "artsy." I would go out with the weirdest color schemes on and the weirdest crazy looks. My hair would be pinned up on one side, and I'd have bright eyeshadow on—a different color every day—and my friends would just say, "That's Falesha!" My mom never looked at me and said not to wear something. Everyone just knew it was me. I rocked my art, expressed myself, and I loved it.

In grades seven and eight, when I was about twelve years old, I started performing with my two friends at recesses and lunch periods in front of my whole elementary school—or at least, whoever wanted to watch us! We would sing Salt n' Peppa, or Mya, or Destiny's Child or Mariah Carey, or Toni Braxton . . . whatever was hot. Even the teachers would watch us!

I loved performing and choreographing routines. We didn't have a
~~~

name. People would introduce us like, "Let's put our hands together for . . . Falesha and her dancers!"

It wasn't a hobby for me. It was what I wanted to do for the rest of my life. Today, one of those same two girls who used to dance in the school-yard with me is a part of my company. She decided to keep dancing. I'm blessed that she's been with me since those first days.

One year, my elementary school decided to put on *Grease* as a concert. I was picked by my teacher to be Sandy. I remember thinking, *I'm not Caucasian. Why would you pick me to be Sandy?* Being of mixed descent, I remember trying to figure out who I was in those years. I wasn't comfortable around all my friends who were simply one ethnic background. Most of my friends were either Caucasian, Spanish, or Black. I was a biracial child; my mother was Filipino, and my father was Jamaican. I struggled during those preteen years to understand my identity amongst the people around me. All I knew was I was a performer.

My teacher said, "Well, you perform anyway in front of everyone every day!" So there I was, in a poodle skirt with Danny, loving every minute. Everyone knew I was a dancer and a singer, so it just seemed to fit. The night of the concert I had chickenpox, but nothing held me back. The show was a hit, I sang my young little heart out and danced the night away.

I found myself performing more frequently, with no prior dance training. I learned quickly that dance was something I was blessed to be able to do fairly naturally. It was easier for me than most of my friends, and certainly my cousins. Of course, as I got older, I learned from the best, but it was at this age that I started to discover there was something natural about it for me. The more I did it, the more I loved it.

Chapter 3

THE DECISION

*Your life changes the moment you make a new,
congruent and committed decision.*
-TONY ROBBINS

I went to three different high schools. I was doing well in school, but I cared about performing more than any subject I was taking.

I remember being super excited to go to New York for a weekend for a modeling opportunity. While I was there, I fell in love with one of their dance schools. When I returned back to Toronto, I continued to go to dance classes and go through the motions; my heart was in the art.

Wanting to start making some of my own money, I started working for my uncle who owned a cleaning business. He had big contracts with companies like Mattamy Homes and other builders, and I ended up working for him for a while. I wanted to be able to buy my own things. I loved shopping for shoes and pretty little dresses, so I worked hard to achieve those goals; I also wanted to be able to help my mom by buying my own bus passes. I was dancing at events like weddings and birthday parties, so costumes started to add up to be another expense. I needed to continually find ways to buy and make costumes. In addition to working for my uncle, I started partnering with friends. If they were running a business, I would offer their business to people as well. So I ended up doing many different things at the same time.

When I turned fifteen, I knew I needed to make dance into something more. I had an entrepreneurial spirit, and I started thinking about what I was going to do after high school and later on in life. I wanted a business card. I got one printed with all of the many things I was doing at the time.

Then one day when I was at home on a lunch break from school, I thought, *I need to have a name for this.* Everyone called me "Diva." I looked at my business card, and I thought of Toronto and the people I was going to serve, and all of the things I was doing. I was using the restroom and I had it on my mind, and as I was washing my hands, all of a sudden it came to me: "Diverse."

My mom was home from work that day, and I ran up to her, excited. "Mom, what do you think of the name, 'Diva Diverse'?"

"Well, you're a diva, and you're diverse. So yeah—it makes sense."

"Perfect. Can we go and register it?"

My mom came with me because I was under eighteen. We went to Service Canada at Scarborough Town Centre. I asked for the cheapest way to register a business. They suggested I become a sole proprietor. I said, "Sole what? Can you write it for me?" I could barely say it. I had never heard of it. I just wanted to be registered so I could open a bank account and start putting money into it. I knew I needed to get money into the company, but I had no idea what I was doing. I just had such a strong drive and motivation to make money dancing and to make a long-term career for myself.

And with that, the company was born.

DIVA DIVERSE

* BELLY DANCING
* LATIN / SALSA
* MODERN / HIP HOP
* DJ'S

* VEHICLES
* MORTGAGES
* CLEANING SERVICES
* OCCASIONS

Falesha Raquel

E-mail: falesharaquel@hotmail.com
www: myspace.com/falesharaquel

I don't know how seriously my mom took me because when it came time for graduation, she said I needed to figure out what I was going to do for university. I told her I was going to be a dancer. She said, "You're not going to New York to be a dancer. You're going to graduate with a degree in dance? Come on." I knew my mom was only trying to look out for me. I thanked her for caring about me. I discovered that year that ballet was not my strength. The school was all ballerinas. I think I may have been the worst ballet dancer *ever*. I would fake my left split. Still today, I reap the consequences of trying to manipulate my teacher into thinking I was doing it correctly because my left leg doesn't reach as high as my right leg. Frustrated one day, I said to my teacher, "I'm not a ballet dancer. I'm more of a belly dancer." She told me I wasn't going to be able to make a career of it and that belly dancers don't make money. She said that "ballet is a requirement" to have a career in dance.

I just thought, *Watch me.*

When I got home after that, I became a ballet teacher for seven years at the YMCA. I knew I wasn't a great ballerina, but I knew the basics, and I got a job teaching it. My family still thought it was just a hobby. I'd hear things like, "You can't make this into a real business," "People aren't going to respect you," and, "You can dance until you're maybe eighteen, but then you're going to have to pull up your socks and go corporate." It was pretty tough to hear all the doubt coming at me from all sides. But it didn't matter. I made a decision that I wanted to make money as a dancer. Period.

Around that time, I started to love belly dancing more and more and found I was practicing it more than any other type of dance. I hadn't ever taken belly dancing lessons; I used to watch music videos and then emulate what I saw in front of the mirror. I liked learning how to dance this way because I was able to learn the basics and make the moves my own at the same time. You might think I was vain for watching myself in the mirror like that, but I looked at the mirror like it was my audience. I think it's how I learned to do certain things with my body on stage that most dancers can't do or haven't even tried. The mirror became my audience. I learned quickly: If it doesn't look good in the mirror, don't do it for the eyes!

As my love for belly dance grew, I started to book my own small gigs on weekends around Toronto where I could showcase it. I loved performing, but I was really taking advantage of when I started. The first restaurant I danced at had me dancing for forty-five minutes straight and paid me seventy-five bucks. I learned quickly that I had to start charging more. I started to realize that it was not worth my time and energy to dance for less than a certain amount. I set that amount as the bar and started only accepting jobs at that rate. I started to realize, *If you don't want me, and you can't afford it, then I'd rather put my energy elsewhere!* It was tough at first, not knowing if they would move forward in booking me. I was forced to develop a bit of a thick skin about the kinds of jobs I would book. Otherwise I wouldn't have succeeded. It really taught my clients the value of my shows.

I had my fair share of not being taken seriously when I tried to open a business bank account. It's not easy to open a bank account in the arts. Being in this field and trying to be a businesswoman can be the biggest shutdown. The first time I walked into the bank, the conversation was embarrassing. I said I was there to open a bank account.

"What kind of bank account?"

"A business account."

"What kind of business are you running?"

"I own a dance company."

I swear they chuckled at me. They may as well have just said it. *What? A dance company opening a bank account?*

I was so naïve. "What's the problem?"

I opened the account anyway because I knew I was going to have cheques coming in, and I needed to be able to keep things organized, but I knew from that moment it was going to be hard. This was just me opening an account for me to put money into the bank, and they were giving me a hard time. I realized it wasn't going to be handed to me. I was going to have to learn to become a businesswoman. I didn't have any entrepreneurial women in my family as role models in this regard, so I had to pretty much figure it out. It was a rough go at first, but I was determined to succeed.

My determination was partly because of my love for dance, and partly because I wanted a better life than the life I saw the people around me had when I was growing up. We lived in a very small community of people who didn't make very much money. One day my good-hearted mom went to drop off our neighbor's lunch at her work, and I happened to be with my mom. We walked through the factory to find our neighbor. I just kept thinking, *This is where you work?* I couldn't believe she worked there. I got upset and asked my mom if I had to go to school so many years, and take exams year after year and work so hard, to work there. I knew in that moment there was no way I could ever work there. I couldn't do it. I would think back to that day when things would get tough, and I knew I *had* to figure it out.

The only option, then, was for me to become a businesswoman if I wanted the business to succeed. I knew I had to start changing.

I started observing other dancers around me who were also trying to make a business of their art. I knew a hip-hop dancer who tried it and unfortunately failed. But I learned from what I thought were his mistakes and tried something different. I would experiment with a few things in my mind and try to play them out to see if they worked.

After I opened my account, I hired someone to help me write a business plan. Next, I started to learn about accounting. I got a new business card done up, and I got a website up and running. My first website was the ugliest site *ever!* It had so much flash it was overwhelming. It was something I wish I had a snapshot of because if I could show you, your eyes would just *bleed.* But it was great for me to explore at the time because I was really making it a business.

I started going to networking events to get more acquainted with the business world. I analyzed everything. I noticed right away that people would dress to impress and would hand you their business card, and that a lot of them had good acting skills. They would introduce themselves a certain way, and when I'd Google them, I'd see they weren't actually doing that well. I started to realize networking events were, for the most part, about marketing.

Everything I was exposed to in those early days was an asset and helped me in my business. I started to learn quickly that if I told people I ran a dance company, they wouldn't take me seriously. When I'd say I own a dance company to a dancer, they'd say, "Oh my gosh, that's *amazing.* How do I dance for you? Are you looking for dancers?" When I'd go into the corporate world with confidence and say the same thing, they'd chuckle and change the subject. Someone actually said to me once, "Oh, it's nice that you can make money prancing around on stage." There is so much more to running a dance company than the dancing itself! I started saying instead that I own a *talent agency.* You'd be surprised how big of a difference this made for most people. People started to respect the business a little bit more.

I had to develop a thickness pretty quickly because I didn't get the response I thought I would get from being a business owner. There were times I would go to an event and be so excited to expose my service, and I would just get *crushed.* I would go home and be upset and think of new ways to fix it.

I had the same issue when I went back to the bank to get a corporate credit card. They immediately said I wouldn't be approved. They told me that what I was doing was art, and that I'd be better to open up a not-for-profit organization and apply for a grant. They wouldn't even approve me for a limit of $1,000.

I couldn't believe it. All I kept thinking was, *This is a dance company. We make money. We do gigs. We do a lot of gigs. How can you not even give me $1,000?* I needed money in order to make more money. I needed to buy costumes, another thing they didn't understand. It was of such little importance to them, but it made all the difference in the world to me when I was trying to really establish the business. I knew I could give all the time in the world to my dancers and teach them, but if they didn't look great on stage doing the choreography because their costumes weren't elaborate, no one would book us. If no one booked us, we wouldn't make money. If we didn't make money, we wouldn't have a business. The bank didn't see it. They told me it was a hobby.

I still knew Diva Diverse was meant to be. So I kept going, trying to find ways to make it work.

Chapter 4

AT FIRST SIGHT

When I saw you, I fell in love, and you smiled because you knew.
-WILLIAM SHAKESPEARE

It was in those early days of the business that I met my husband. One day, when I was in my early teens, I made a promise to my grandfather. I said to him, "I'm going to be okay. Don't worry about me. I'm going to wait." I knew my grandparents were holding their breath when I turned seventeen because that was the age my mom was pregnant with me, and my aunt was also pregnant at seventeen with my cousin. I was next! And there I was, seventeen, and I had a boyfriend. You can just imagine the anticipation.

I don't think there's anything wrong with being pregnant young, as long as you're ready to be a parent. Pregnancy is a beautiful thing. But I, in particular, was not ready at seventeen to start a family. I knew that, so I made sure my grandparents knew I knew that as well. I had big dreams I wanted to pursue with Diva Diverse, even if I didn't know exactly what they all looked like just yet. I said to my grandfather, "Grandpa, didn't I tell you that I was going to be successful? How can I run a business if I have a kid at this age? I have a lot to do first." I sure knew it was possible to be successful even if I did have a kid young, however, I just didn't wanna make it harder on myself.

He looked at me, half in disbelief, and said, "Oh yeah—okay," with his thick Filipino accent.

I read between the lines to gather that he really wasn't sure about my statement and didn't know what else to say. I think he wanted me to show him, *really*, that I was going to be successful.

Although my business was my first focus at that point, I did have a clear vision that I wanted to be married right away. I used to write about it in my diary. When I was about thirteen years old, there was this one page where I wrote "My Ideal Husband" at the top and was very particular in writing out the details. My favorite toys when I was a kid were Barbie and Ken. Barbie had a pink Jeep, and Ken had a green truck. I used to love changing her girly clothes and combing her hair. I used to think, *When I get older, I want to be Barbie and Ken, but we're going to be the ethnic version.*

I remember every detail. I wrote that my husband was going to have long hair and caramel skin, a little darker than mine. He was going to have abs and muscles, and he was going to be taller than me. He would have a good job and his driver's license. And every single guy I dated when I was fourteen to seventeen, I would hold up to my ideal husband. I would ask them questions like, "So does your mom give you an allowance? Do you drive? As I got older, the questions evolved to things like, "Did you finish school?" "Do you have any kids?" I used to interview everyone!

I first saw Shane as he was walking past me at Toronto's well known Caribana, also known as Carnival. I saw him, but he didn't notice me. I was with two of my girlfriends, and we were walking and singing Beyoncé songs at the top of our lungs. Shane was walking with his friends, and I pointed him out to my girlfriends. They thought he was handsome and told me I should go talk to him, introduce myself, and feel him out. I thought maybe he was from the States, perhaps there was no point as I wasn't in for a long-distance relationship should something work out. Plus, I wanted him to notice me first.

So at it I went, letting my hair blow in the wind and being in a zone of thinking I was in the middle of a Pantene Pro-V commercial, I slowly looked over at him, and . . .

He didn't notice me.

I ended up spending the entire rest of the night talking about him. I was teaching dance at the YMCA at the time and also working at their front desk. I talked about him to all the staff for four weeks. They were so annoyed from hearing about this guy who I would never see again.

One day at the Y, I was talking to Rosie, one of the girls, about how I was stressed out. I needed to find a DJ to help me put together a Beyoncé mix for a big event I was performing at, and it was coming up very soon. The event was only two months away, and there was still so much work to do. She took one look at me and said, "Girl, don't worry. I have a DJ for you. He comes here to work out. He'll take care of you."

Half an hour later, Shane walked through the door of the YMCA.

"Oh Fee, remember the DJ I was talking about?"

I'd already seen him. I ran to the bathroom. I had to leave the front desk.

Rosie ran in. "He's right there—you have to go talk to him. Why did you run off?"

"Rosie, you know that guy I've been telling you about? The guy I fell in love with at first sight?"

"Yeah . . . the guy from the Carnival . . . how can I forget? You've been talking about him for weeks."

"It's *him.*"

"No way!" She started freaking out, and I swear it was like the whole YMCA came into the bathroom. All the staff were so interested in what was going on and why we were yelling.

It took me twenty minutes to pull myself together. I tried to grow up to be able to go talk to him. He was ten years older than me, and at that point I just turned nineteen.

He had already started working out, so when I finally could hold my composure long enough, I walked up to him and said, in probably the dorkiest way ever, "Hi, Shane, Rosie tells me you're a DJ. I'm a dancer. And a singer. I was just wondering if you could make a mix for me."

He kept lifting and glanced over at me. "Yeah, what do you need?" in a macho-type mannerism.

As we started talking, I could see my whole life with him. He was talking, and I was in dreamland, picturing our future together in between saying, "Uh huh . . . uh huh . . . " enough times so he wouldn't pick up on it and think I was weird.

The only thing I heard was, "You can come to my house so I can make the mix for you."

What? "I can come to your house? Really?! Okay . . ." I couldn't believe it. One minute I was talking to everyone I knew about a guy who didn't notice me at the carnival. The next minute I was going to his house. *What?!*

He wrote his address on a piece of scrap paper. I was on cloud nine for the rest of the night.

A week later, he made my mix. I invited him to my show, and he watched me perform with all my dancers, and he said he really liked it. I knew I wanted to spend more time with him, and he seemed up for it too. He invited me to one of his DJ gigs. I was, of course, excited to go.

The night of his event came, and I was super pumped. Naturally, I spent the entire time out on the dance floor. I was so impressed with how he mixed the songs. His playlist was amazing. Everything I was learning about Shane made me like him even more.

As we spent more time together, I remembered what my grandparents had told me: that if I pay too much attention to a guy when we're dating, he'll stop being interested and stop calling me. I started to wonder if that was going to happen. I certainly hadn't held myself back from trying to spend as much time with him as I could. He didn't call one night, and I started to worry that I had appeared desperate or something. I thought I blew it.

Then that night, at maybe 1:00 in the morning, he messaged me saying that Halloween was around the corner and he wanted to invite me over to his house to hand out candy with him.

I legitimately threw my phone in the air with excitement. I couldn't believe it! I ran to my mom's room.

"Mom, he messaged me!"

My mom didn't understand. "What do you mean? Of course he was going to message you. You guys have been spending lots of time together."

"No, you don't get it! I've already been to his house and I've been to his events and I like him so much and I'm sure he knows it and he's still talking to me!" I thought for sure he wouldn't care by that point. It seemed as though men would get what they wanted and move on to the next girl. But he invited me to hand out candy to the kids with him. I was over the hill excited, as you could imagine.

A few months later, he gave me a Valentine's Day card that said, *I love you so much. This is the key to my heart.* There was a key to his house in the card. I moved in, and the rest was history.

He was everything I had written in my diary. I even wrote about my wedding in my diary, and our wedding was everything I had imagined. I wrote that I wanted to be married young, on a beach barefoot, on some tropical island with my bridal party wearing baby pink, to my perfect husband. I got married at twenty-two; our cruise docked, and we got married on a sandy beach in Jamaica, my bridesmaids were in baby pink short gowns with diamonds, and the guys were in white and pink suits. It was everything I had dreamed of.

Our wedding was even talked about on the radio. I was a pageant queen at that time, so the media talked about it, wrote about it, and put it was on YouTube. I was Miss Caribbean, and I had won Beauties of Asia earlier that year. It was a great time in my life. I loved it so much. I was so grateful and humbled by all the support in my life.

Somehow, I didn't carry the trauma of sexual abuse I had experienced in my childhood into adulthood. I remember when I was growing up, I used to hear people talk about Oprah and her situation, and other women's situations. I would hear that a woman who goes through something like that in her childhood usually grows up having an issue in relationships. I don't know why that didn't happen to me. It could possibly be because

I was so determined as a young adult to marry young and to find a good man. If anything, it had the effect of helping me see what kind of man I wanted to be with.

In the early years of our marriage, it came up in conversation somehow. He was questioning me about my past. (Trust me—I had done my fair share of interviewing him about his past when we first met!) I finally told him about it, four years into our marriage.

He was so great about it. He looked at me with compassion and said, "Wow. I never knew that about you. That's terrible you had to go through that."

I said, "Why would I talk about it?"

"Well, to heal, I guess. But I would have never thought anything like that happened. Why are you okay?"

"What do you mean?" I didn't understand.

"You went through sexual abuse—you realize that, right?"

"Yeah—I guess it was sexual abuse, yeah." I had never really thought of it in those terms before.

"So why are you okay? You don't seem wounded or closed off at all."

"I don't know." I genuinely didn't know what to say. All I knew is that I turned away from that time in my life and started writing about the way I wanted my life to be. My dairy became my best friend, and writing became how I healed anything from my past. I released all of it through writing.

That's why I put such an emphasis on writing in this book. In Part Two, there is room for you to write about your thoughts and your life. I encourage you to use that space to jot things down when you get there. If you're not a writer, or you haven't written in a long time, don't worry. You don't have to be good at writing for writing to be a healing process. Just jot your thoughts down. You might be surprised about what you find when you put pen to paper.

My cousins, who went through the abuse with me when we were young, ask me now how I knew Shane was a good choice. They say to me, "You picked the perfect husband. How did you know?" We really aren't perfect; no one is. We just work it out. I say to them, "I didn't pick him, I manifested him." My mom loves him so much. They get along so well. He treats my mom as if she were his. If she needs something fixed on her car, he's right there to help. Whatever the family needs, they can always call Shane. He's a blessing to our whole family, and one that I will be eternally grateful for.

He was also so great about supporting the business. After we got married, I couldn't afford a real dance studio. We lived in a small-sized bungalow, our house wasn't very big, but we did have extra space. I thought, finally I had my own space with my husband, we had no kids, what was I going to do with the house? What's the only thing a woman like me who loves the arts would do? Have my own costume closet.

My father-in-law made one of our bedrooms a costume closet for all my dance stuff. It seemed like one of the best things that had ever happened in my life. He installed racks all over the room with LED lights, and I hung out all my belly dance costumes, all my Brazilian costumes with big feather-head dresses, all of the costumes I had at that time. I already had quite a lot of costumes at that point. The girls would come over, and we would practice in the backyard, on the driveway or inside facing the mirror. And that's where we would get ready to do shows. It was simple, but it worked. And Shane was great about all of it.

Chapter 5

THE PATH OF LEAST RESISTANCE

*People hate what they don't understand
and fear what they can't conquer.*
-PITBULL

*You've got to take risks if you're going to succeed. I would
much rather ask forgiveness than permission.*
-RICHARD BRANSON

Unfortunately, due to the financial pressures I faced in those early days, I ended up getting sucked back into society. I had made the decision to start the company, and I was booking gigs and teaching dance, and then something hit me one day. And this happens to everyone at some point. I woke up one morning and did an inventory of my friends and the people I knew. I saw they were all making money working corporate jobs. I knew I was an artsy person, but I also knew I needed to make money, and things weren't happening fast enough. I started playing the deadly *what-if* game in my head. *What if I never get funding from the bank? What if I can't afford to pay my dancers next month? What if.* It was distracting, and I got pretty distressed about it.

So I got a job at the Bank of Montreal. My mom was certainly happy! It took the pressure off Shane as well. We were newly married, and I didn't want to add financial stress to his plate.

It was great to be able to pay my bills with no second thought. There was relief in that sense, but it didn't last long. Within a couple of years, I started going to the bathroom in the middle of my shifts. I would lock myself in a stall and cry. I would get back out on the floor and try to act like everything was fine.

I would get home every night and just be miserable. I dreaded having to go back the next day. I'd say to Shane, "I can't do this. How do people do it? How do people have jobs like this for fifteen years and have no problem with it?" It was agonizing for me.

I had had a few jobs before that. I had tried a few things because I wanted to make money. I bounced around from job to job because I was trying to figure out what made me happy. I wanted to be excited to go to work. I first started working when I was living with my mom, which was perfect because I didn't have to pay rent. I was only paying for my cell phone bill, which was about thirty dollars a month. But at the time, it seemed a lot that I needed to be responsible for making sure that I had thirty dollars every month! So I started working young.

Working retail at Le Chateau was my very first job. I was in grade nine. We worked on salary plus commission, and I needed to sell something every day to keep my job. I was surprised to find out that was how some retail stores did things. I had no idea! It was stressful, having to sell something all the time and having a boss on my back asking me if I had made quota every day. I was so young, and I didn't want to force people to buy things. I didn't even last my three months' probation. I went in one day and my name was not on the schedule, and I never showed up again. Even though I didn't like the job, I was pretty upset. My feelings would get hurt so easily back then.

Next, I worked at a shoe store in Dufferin Mall. I liked that job a little more because I got 90 percent off all shoes in the store. Did I mention how much I love shoes? That's when my shoe fetish was born! It didn't take me long to have a whole closet of shoes.

I was seventeen when I started working at the YMCA. I started by volunteering once a week, and they loved what I was teaching, so they started paying me a small wage. I was so happy I was getting paid to teach dance lessons! I started teaching a ballet class at first, which grew to a very popular adult Latin class, and then that increased to twice a week; eventually, I created a whole dance program. I called it "divacise." I also started to help out at the daycare. I loved teaching dance during the week and childminding every weekend.

I learned how to teach through dancing with other dance companies, and I would just pick things up. I learned the names of the steps of a few different types of dance. Then I would go and teach my class with an enhanced repertoire.

I had a minimum of twenty kids in each of my classes: all these little princesses in their leotards and tutus. After a little while of teaching ballet, they asked me if I knew anything about hip hop and if I could teach a class on that as well. So I started to teach hip hop.

Then I started teaching an adult class for a few semesters because the Y wanted to try it out. The adults were more drawn towards Latin dance, but eventually I introduced them to Bollywood and belly dance. I started changing my classes and learning more styles to be able to offer what people wanted or what they were curious about. Over the course of a few short months, I created a whole dance program for them too. By that point, I was working five days a week and was making good money teaching. I loved my YMCA life.

In time, I decided to start working at McDonalds as well. When I tell people I worked at McDonalds, they look at me and say, "You're so diva, and you worked at McDonald's?" But it was the job that taught me more about responsibility and the idea that you can make as much money as you put into your work because while I was working there, I managed to buy my first car.

I bought a standard car because it was less expensive than an automatic. Everyone wondered how I was going to learn to drive standard. I was determined to learn because I didn't want to pay more than I needed to. I loved that it was cheaper, but it started to ruin all of those high heels I had. I'd gotten 90 percent off all of my gorgeous shoes, and they were all going to get ruined? No way.

More importantly, I needed an automatic car because my grandfather got diagnosed with cancer around that time, and he hated my sports car. I drove him to his chemotherapy appointments twice a week. I didn't want him to have to take a taxi, and my grandparents didn't drive—my grandmother had never driven, and my grandfather wasn't able to drive since he'd had triple bypass surgery. Every time I would change the clutch, it would make a *"nerrrrrrrr"* sound. It made him nervous. So I knew I needed a new car. Don't get me wrong; my handling of a standard car is pretty smooth.

My grandfather did tell me at one point that when he first came to Canada from the Philippines, he got a Chevy hatch-back. As soon as I laid my eyes on a Malibu Chevrolet hatchback at the dealership, I fell in love. It was exactly what my grandfather had owned, just a newer version. I was excited thinking about how much he was going to love it.

I financed it. I was eighteen at the time and didn't know anything about business or the art of negotiation. I got ripped off so badly. A car that I thought was $21,000 turned out to be $50,000 by the time I paid it off. They gave me an interest rate of 17 percent because I was only eighteen and hadn't established my credit yet. Fair—I get that I didn't have credit built up, so it was higher risk for them. But it was wildly irresponsible for them to sell me the car in the first place. The man who sold me the car just wanted the sale, regardless of the financial position it was putting me in.

I was upset with myself for not understanding business and making a bad decision. It motivated me to learn about the business of selling cars and to get inside the mind of the man who had sold me the car. I really couldn't understand how someone could do something like that to a kid. I applied to work at the dealership, took the required exam to become licensed, and got the job. I left McDonalds and started learning about the car business.

I quickly learned a lot about the business. I'm a guy when it comes to cars. I can tell you about the horsepower, the torque, the engine, the parts. I loved it. At twenty, I became the number-one car salesperson in my district for a duration of time. They featured me in the *Auto Mart* magazine. I was this young girl, dressed like a young girl, standing beside these businessmen in suits. Thinking back, I don't even know how I got hired. I didn't have any business sense. I didn't understand how to be professional back then. The most important thing I did have, however, was motivation.

I worked my butt off to pay off that car because I didn't want to disappoint my mom. I still had the car when Shane and I got married, and he helped me pay it off. If it wasn't for him, I would have been paying it off until I was twenty-six. My insurance was also high to start because I didn't go to driving school. Funny enough, we now own one. We named it Driving Skills Academy.

I never told the man who had sold me the car that it was irresponsible of him to sell it to me. I didn't have the courage to say it to him. He looked like Spartacus. He was *huge*. There was no way at the time I could say that to a 200-pound Russian businessman.

He ended up quitting after I started working there and opening his own dealership. I found out years later that his dealership went bankrupt. He was scamming many people who didn't know any better. He actually sold a Mercedes to my mom. We figured out one day while we were having breakfast together. She said, "I really don't like the guy who sold me this car. I feel like I'm being overcharged." When I asked her to describe him, she said, "I think he is some kind of European or something." We Googled him, and it was the same guy. Anyway, he went bankrupt a short time after.

Working at the dealership I grew to like working for a commission (a far cry from my early days at Le Chateau). I started thinking about ways I could make a larger commission and started to develop a love for real estate, so I got my mortgage license. I was still dancing and teaching dance at the YMCA. But I was always eager to find additional ways to cultivate more revenue streams because the banks weren't funding my company, and the company wasn't making enough money on its own. I educated myself by reading many different books to help guide me along the way.

Eventually, I grew tired from having to hustle so much for the money I needed. I even did some telemarketing here and there after school. Even when I was still living at home, I always had two or three jobs, trying to make enough money to pay for my expensive car. After I was married, the business still wasn't making enough money. That's when a full-time job became a pretty attractive option.

So we come full circle: I ended up working at the bank. I was relieved that at least I could work in one place and make enough money to sustain my lifestyle. I worked there full time for two years. It felt like forever. And that's when my back was up against the wall. I was still dancing after every shift, either in rehearsal with Diva Diverse or at work for the YMCA. I was still dancing *in* the business (and very little at that), but I didn't have much time to spend *on* my business. It was suffocating.

What finally pushed me over the edge was when I realized I was stuck in a routine of growing someone else's company instead of putting that time into growing my own. I only had time for Diva Diverse for a few hours when the sun went down and I was already exhausted from closing deals at the bank. I would see the numbers I was bringing in for the bank and then look at what they were paying me. I couldn't live with it. My quota per quarter as a teller was just ridiculous, but I was stuck making a fixed salary.

The truth is, that's business, and I understand and love business. I get it. If someone buys something for thirty cents and sells it for ten dollars, that's business. I understand that's how business works. But I couldn't live with it at the bank because I knew I wasn't meant to put my time and energy into supporting someone else's business—I knew I was supposed to build out my own. I knew I needed to leave, but I felt stuck. I was worried about money. This is when I started hiding in the bathroom stalls every day, in tears.

It started to put a strain on my marriage. Shane was DJing still at that point and would leave for an event as I would come home from a shift. We were like sliding doors. We were newlyweds, and I couldn't believe that was what our marriage was like. I wondered, *Is this how people live? Do we just both work hard to pay for a mortgage later on and get pregnant . . . is this it?*

Shane was so happy when I got the job at BMO. He could tell his family his wife worked in a bank! When I would come home unhappy, he would say, "Well, this is life." His mom was a law clerk, and his dad worked hard in construction and they could afford a big house. But I would remind him that I was built differently. I wanted to be happy in my career, but I just needed to find a way.

I started to feel really not myself. I went to the doctor, and he put me on a heart monitor to see if something was wrong with my heart because heart problems run in my family. I went into work with a heart monitor one day, and they encouraged me to take a short-term stress leave. I was off work for three months. They continued to pay me a portion of my salary.

I went for a second and third opinion, and all of the doctors I saw told me I was healthy. My heart was checked on an ultrasound, and everything was fine. I finally went to a holistic doctor who told me the reason I felt that way was likely because I wasn't happy and I needed to change something in my life. It stuck with me. He said our minds are the most complex computers in the world, and if we fill them with things we are truly not happy with, it's going to show in our bodies somehow. He said I needed to stop, go home, and get some rest; he encouraged me to meditate. It was good advice.

I did just that. I rested and got my energy back up. And during those three months, I did everything under the sun to get Diva Diverse to a point where it was able to pay me some money. I taught private lessons to new brides who were getting ready for their first dance. I taught people who just wanted to learn how to do some dance moves for whatever they needed. I picked up more shifts at the YMCA so I was working in the daytime as well. I started putting my marketing together, saying, "Hire us for your next event." The business started to grow, and I hired two of my friends to help me.

At the end of the three-month stress leave, I gave my notice. I haven't left Diva Diverse since.

There have been pockets since then that I have thought about getting a job again if it's slow, but now I understand business goes up and down, and I prepare for it. If when business went down I were to get a job again, I would never be able to bring business back up because I would be focused on the job. And I realized after going through it myself that this is why people fail. So I actually brace myself for that low time now, and I make sure I have my money right in advance.

Now, when I look at the business, sometimes I can't believe how many people it pays: about sixty different dancers in a year, two assistants, one manager, an accountant, my lawyer, and me. It wasn't easy building it to this point and having what I needed along the way in order to do so, but I was blessed with an opportunity to take action and I did. With a vengeance. The business has been my number one ever since, and now it gives me everything I need.

It truly gives dancers an opportunity to grow and a chance to explore all dance styles.

I'm so grateful.

Chapter 6

MAMA DIVA

Whatever good things we build end up building us.
-JIM ROHN

I certainly learned during that three-month blitz how to be persistent. I really believe now that *anything* can work with persistence and motivation. If I hadn't been motivated to get the business off the ground during my time off, nothing would have changed. If I hadn't been motivated to leave the bank, I'd still be there. Leaving was the first step to having to make it. I didn't have a safety net anymore. And it was the best thing for me. It was what forced me to grow into a true businesswoman. From there, I was persistent at making sure I could make the dance company an actual sustainable business.

I was exposed to multi-level marketing around that time, and it helped me a great deal. I benefited from the exposure to a successful business model. Someone I knew who had an ACN business brought me to a meeting. They said the sign-up fee to begin an ACN business was $500, and after that they would support us with a full back-end website and system. All we had to do was sell the service. While the rest of the people in the room were thinking about starting an ACN business, I was sitting there thinking about how I could apply what I was learning to Diva Diverse.

Excited about the idea of setting up a similar business model, one of the first things I did was create introduction videos. I wanted Diva Diverse to be an international company, and I knew I wasn't going to be able to meet with everyone on the team face-to-face. I wasn't just interested in running a dance company; Diva Diverse was going to be a *lifestyle.* I made an orientation video for my dancers to watch when they were accepted into the company after auditions. It was me saying, "If you're watching this video right now, I want to introduce myself. My name is Falesha Raquel, the owner of Diva Diverse. Congratulations and welcome to the team." I went into the contract, what my expectations were, how I was going to support them, and anything else they needed to know. I made a second, back-end video for agents of the company and people making commission for booking events. I started with a few agents after that and that helped to get the company more bookings.

The ACN meeting I went to started to work on me. It started to change my mind and the way I was thinking. People started paying monthly fees to be part of my company, and I would provide them costumes, and costume maintenance and preparation. I started being able to fund more costumes, which improved our shows. My home closet of costumes grew to well over a hundred within a few months. I kept surrounding myself with business, and reading a lot. Instead of going out partying like my friends, I spent most of my time trying to figure out how I was going to make Diva Diverse better and bigger.

As the company grew, I needed a bigger space for my dancers and me to rehearse. Our house wasn't big enough anymore. We were busy, but I still couldn't afford a dance studio full time. So what did I do? I made a dance studio in a flea market. It was the most unlikely spot for a dance studio *ever*. But we did it.

I called all the flea markets around to see who could offer the cheapest rent. I decided to go with the Keele and Sheppard market. I rented a little square of space in the market. I quickly realized I needed more space, so I rented two booths beside each other. I asked my father-in-law to fill the space with mirrors and good flooring.

I found a good supplier and set up a little jewelry section so people could buy jewelry as well, and had a dance section where people could come in for classes and book our services. We started rehearsing there for shows. My father-in-law lined the dance space with big, beautiful burgundy curtains so the girls would feel safe and secure rehearsing in private.

We were only open when the flea market was open—on Saturdays and Sundays. I would get up early on Saturdays and Sundays after performing and go open my studio. It was humble beginnings, but the point was I had a dance studio. I didn't care if it was in a market and only open two days a week.

People would come for dance classes and then shop at the flea market. We were right in the food court area, so there were always people around. We would put on little shows when we didn't have classes going on.

The studio looked like royalty had just popped up out of nowhere. Everything else at the flea market was so grungy. You know how flea markets are. But we were divas. There were diamonds laid out and bling jewelry for sale. Even the floor was burgundy. It worked. It was exactly what we needed.

We booked a lot of shows that way. A lot of women were drawn to the jewelry. As they were buying jewelry and talking to me, I would upsell the company. I would ask them if they'd ever thought of hiring dancers for anything. It wasn't something many people were familiar with. I'd say, "If you ever have a birthday party, or someone you know is getting married, or for your anniversary party." I got the company exposure every chance I got. If they didn't know of any events they could hire us for, I'd offer belly dancing classes. We got a lot of clients that way.

I was there in that little makeshift studio for a good year and a half. It was perfect. A decade later, they still have my mirrors up. I love going by to visit now and remembering back to my first studio.

There was a point when I realized we had to leave. We weren't selling the business as much, I wasn't selling as much jewelry, the air started to get a bit stale, the bathrooms a bit dirty, and people weren't watching our dancing as much. It was time to make a move.

Out of nowhere, one of my girlfriends called me up one day and said, "I know you have a dance studio in a flea market, and I know you live in Scarborough, but my husband and I wanted to reach out to you and make you an offer to share our industrial space." Her husband had a space where he ran a business that supplied businesses with takeout supplies. It was a 3000-square-foot space and they had an open space between their industrial business area at the back and their office at the front. "Pay me $400 a month, or whatever you're paying at the flea market."

"Done."

I put up dividers so when our clients would walk in, they wouldn't see all of their supplies, they would walk straight into my dance studio. I had the time of my life. I auditioned girls there, we had rehearsals . . . I was on the *grind*. At that time, we didn't have a lot of competition because dance companies weren't really doing what we were doing. I ran a kids' camp there from 8:30 in the morning to 4:30 in the afternoon. I taught the kids Hawaiian dance, Belly dance, Bollywood, and all different genres. The kids were as young as four and five years old, to as old as twelve years old. After dance camp, in the evenings, I would teach adults. On the weekends, we were performing. If I wasn't performing in Toronto, I was getting gigs in New York. We had more than twenty dancers. I had girls who would graduate from university with dance degrees apply to Diva Diverse.

We were busy, busy, busy.

I started learning how to separate my role as entertainer and my role as business owner with clients. It was challenging to be a businesswoman and an entertainer at the same time. I'd be half naked on stage in a belly dance costume, and then I'd go negotiate the next contract. I was originally going to call this book *Belly Dance and Business* because the two things are like polar opposites—night and day.

When I was the entertainer, I had to play the fun role. I had to be different at night than I was during the day when I'd answer the phone. As the entertainer, I would bring the energy to the stage no matter what. That was what I was paid to do. I could have been having crazy cramps from my monthly visitor or have a cold, and I couldn't let anyone know it. I was there solely for the client and for the audience. The focus was 120 percent on giving them what they wanted. As the businesswoman, I had to change that a bit and have some posture with the client in order to negotiate good deals and contracts. It took me some time to learn how to go back and forth.

In time, I had to learn how to wear many different hats at the same time: I was the talent, the CEO, the administration, the manager of the dancers, and the booking agent for my company. I would spend all night on stage performing, then wake up the next morning and sit in business meetings with banks and investors. I hired and trained my team myself. I signed my own cheques, sought out and rented studios, taught dance, choreographed all of our routines, and practiced every day to keep improving as a dancer.

I was also the optics and marketing in the social media world for the company. I started to see I needed to do things for the fans, things that people were going to like. I would take pictures on beaches, everyday shenanigans, post videos of snippets of our day or even myself and the divas in the studio rehearsing. It kept Diva Diverse on people's minds.

Underneath it all, I was determined to stay a real person. I still am. I know my true self, and I know I'm not really that self-centered, although it can easily be perceived that way. I want to help people. I want to give a lot. I love to donate. I love to help women build their self-esteem. I know I'm not a naive sex symbol. I'm an entertainer, and I do it for my clients and fans. So I learned I had to have different personas in different situations.

I also started thinking about what kind of company I wanted to run. And I don't just mean the vision I had for it being an international company—I was already clear on that. I mean, I started thinking about what I wanted the company to be for everyone who was a part of it.

Growing up being blessed with the talent of being able to perform in front of an audience, I really tried to stay humble because I knew where I came from. And I tried to carry that humility forward as the business grew. I decided I would be present and be my best for every single dancer who I crossed paths with or who joined the company. I wanted to try to build every single one of my dancers to be the best that they could be. I really cared about every single person who joined Diva Diverse. I spent my time with them and gave them as much as I could. My dancers started calling me "Mama Diva." I would always tell them, "Guys, I'm not your mom—I'm the same age as you." But they felt like I was older because I used to have little pep talks with them reminding them to be humble about the fact we were all blessed to be able to do what we were doing. I'd somewhat mentor them on life, marriage, and finances.

I had always been into beauty pageants, and I started coaching pageant girls to help them prepare for shows. I coached a lot of my girls as well, in order to help them build their confidence. I judged a lot of pageants too. I stopped doing pageants because I was married—that was a restriction that they put into effect—and I just naturally lost the desire to compete. But I wanted the other girls to succeed. Pageants help to build confidence, and they help girls network and market the things they're doing. I would tell the girls to think about their purpose for wanting to be in the pageant. What did they want it to help them accomplish in their lives? I loved coaching them. It was natural for me. I felt like a young female version of Tony Robbins.

I also tried to help my girls see how important it was for them to be genuine. I'd remind them it was a privilege to be able to make money dancing; that it was a blessing. I didn't want anyone to take the company for granted. I wanted to show them that it wasn't just a lucky opportunity. I used to say, "Guys, how many of you have really been in dance from the time you were three or four years old, and had your parents paying for your lessons the whole way?" Most of their hands would go up. "And how many of the dancers who were in the same position growing up can actually at the end of it say they make $200 at the end of a fifteen-minute show? Very, very few." I would remind them the company was giving them an opportunity to create a career out of their art. I wanted to make sure they knew the company was a blessing for all of us and that they didn't take it for granted.

I started to get upset when I'd see the dancers come to shows and be so nonchalant about what they were doing. It caused some friction between me and a few of the dancers at times because they didn't understand why I would take things so seriously. They would say, "Well, you're the business owner. We don't look at it the way you do, and we don't have to." And I'd say there was some truth to that, in that the reputation of the business lay on my shoulders; but it was more that I was upset they were given the opportunity to do what they loved and weren't taking it seriously. I didn't understand why they wouldn't give it their all. Why weren't they excited to put on their lashes, makeup, glitter, stockings and costume, do their hair, and perform their all for the next fifteen to twenty minutes. I didn't get it because to me, that was everything. I loved it. People say they want to be JLo and Beyoncé, but are they willing to do what it takes to perform like that? And not just be like them for a twenty-minute show, but live their lifestyle? I encouraged my dancers to be dancers, through and through.

Making a career of dance is different from doing it as a job. We did a lot of local shows. Even when I would go to the grocery store, people started to recognize me. I didn't dress up to be a belly dancer on stage and then come off stage and be someone else. *I was a belly dancer.* It's who I was everywhere. The only difference was I was walking into Walmart wearing street clothes. A lot of my dancers didn't feel that way. When they were on stage, they were a dancer. When they were off stage, they were "normal." I used to tell them they were dancers all the time, but they didn't understand.

I started to realize around that time that there was a difference between a dancer and a performer. There are a lot of dancers out there—so many. And I love dancers. But not every dancer is a *performer*. I saw that I could give someone what they thought was my best show, and I may not have thought it was my best show. I may have been under the weather that day. But I would still perform for them. I would connect with the audience and focus on who was in the room, making eye contact with everyone I could. I would generate enough energy to make the audience feel what I was trying to display as a performer. I learned that I couldn't expect that from every dancer I hired. Not all of them were interested in taking their dancing to the level of performance. It's like saying the sun and other stars are the same. Stars are amazing, and we love them. But it takes a little bit more effort to be as big as the sun. I used to ask my girls to give me more than just "one-two-three-four choreography." Anyone can do that. I used to ask them to give me a *performance*.

Some people never learn the difference, and I believe that's a big reason they don't excel in their careers. As a dancer, you're always competing with a million dancers. I used to say to my girls, "I only need three performers." It's what makes the difference between the corps de ballet and the soloist.

But it takes time. It takes a little more seasoning and a little more finessing to be a performer. This is how I started to make sense of the difference when I would see it.

I continued to write in my diary through these years of growing the business. I believe my diary is one of the main reasons I am the woman I am today. I journaled my life right from my early days, learning things about myself in my writing along the way.

I was a child when I first started writing, and I didn't know at the time how it was going to impact me as a woman, a dancer and businesswoman. I originally started a diary because I saw my mom writing poetry in a journal and I wanted to do the same. If I saw her writing, I would pick up a pencil and open my book as well.

I started with things like, "Dear diary, today my brother and I are fighting." It was pretty silly stuff at first. Then as I grew up, it became things like, "Dear diary, this boy I saw today, I think he likes me. He kissed me on the forehead, and his name is Dane." As I started to mature, I would write things like, "Dear diary, I'm really hoping I can own my own business. I saw in an article that Oprah said . . ." Then it was, "Dear diary, I would like to get married," and "Dear diary, I hope to get pregnant." I would write every night. And as I got older, my writing turned into outlining of goals: "September 15, 2001. Dear diary, these are my goals. I want to . . ."

I looked back at my diary recently and remembered I wrote that when I turn thirty, I need to write a book. I had completely forgotten I had written that. The funny thing was, I had already started writing this book when I saw it in my diary. And I started when I was thirty years old.

There are so many things I wrote as goals over the years, down to things like having fluffy Pomeranians as dogs. Nothing happened overnight. I didn't get my dogs when I was fifteen or sixteen years old, around the time I wrote that. I got them when I was twenty-three. But I still got my doggies.

So writing was always a pretty important part of my life, and during this time of building out the business, it was no different.

As more girls joined the business, I learned how to dance more styles of dance, and we started doing all kinds of performances and events. I continued to be mostly self-taught. I got thrown on stage to do a flamenco piece once, and I'd never taken flamenco. I learned Chinese fan dance and Scottish Highland dance by looking at the style and understanding it. I didn't even know why I understood the different genres or why I was interested in them—they're not my culture, but I liked them anyway.

When we expanded our repertoire of what kinds of performances we could offer, I decided to start offering our services to seniors' homes. There was a personal reason for that as well.

It was 2008, and my grandfather's health was declining. My grandparents were always number one for me. They had a list of all the things I needed to do in order for me to be successful in their eyes, and I made sure I did every single one of the things on that list. The only thing I haven't done yet is have a child, but that's a topic for a future chapter.

My grandfather was living in a senior home at the time because he needed a lot of support for his health. He said to me one day when I went to visit him, "Oh, darling, you're always dancing, but you never dance for me. How am I going to get to see you dance?"

Instinctively, I said, "Well, I guess I'll have to dance here!"

He loved the idea.

But then I started to wonder about how to actually make it happen. It wasn't as easy as it sounded. I spoke to the organizers, and they said, "We're a senior home—we need to get this passed," and there was something that had to be checked with the Ministry of Health . . . there was a lot of paper-work and many delays. It was all corporate stuff. And there I was, a dancer knowing nothing about that space. I had to give them time to approve it.

My grandfather passed away while we were waiting. I was devastated.

We got approved shortly after, and we did our first performance at his senior home. The residents loved it. I think they felt happy that someone cared enough about them to want to perform for them.

Over a decade later, we go back to that home all the time and dance. That home is where he took his last breath. It's always special to me. Now we're in 300 homes.

I just love seniors. I don't even know what it is. It's probably because of my grandparents. I love meeting them. There are so many times I've gone and met seniors at performances, and then I go back to perform and see that person's "in memory of" picture on the wall. And I say to myself, *At least they got to see a show. At least I got to meet them. At least I could give them happiness for that period of time.* I love them. Hopefully we'll double our numbers and have 600 homes one day.

Next, I really started to see the diversity growing in the company. We were really living up to our name. People were calling to book me specifi-cally, but they didn't know my background. They'd say, "Hi, I want to hire the mixed girl. I don't know what she is—is she Latina?" or I'd hear, "Is she Black?" "Is she Indian?" "Is she Mexican?" "Is she Asian?" They were always confused. Every client's perception of me was different.

Sometimes people were specific with the background of the dancers they were hiring because of a particular style of dance. They wanted the cultural background. Because I couldn't do every show myself and I wanted to highlight my dancers, I would tell them that I had another mixed girl for them, or if they said I looked Latina, I would say I had another Latina for them. If they thought I was Black, I would say I had a Black girl for them. When we did shows with a few of us at once, our clients would see girls from all different backgrounds. I started hearing that people liked that we were all from different backgrounds. I started to see that the company really reflected Canada, and we were really living up to our name. We were Diva *Diverse*, after all. Not only did we do all different styles of dance, but we had dancers from all over the world.

In time, at every event, I had every culture on stage. On St. Patty's Day, they weren't just Irish girls. We had Chinese girls dancing, Black girls dancing, Latina girls dancing . . . people loved it. And the girls loved it even more.

With the business rolling, I started looking for more ways I could perform. I was a performer first and then a dancer. Naturally, I wanted to try singing to add to the ways I could perform. I always thought about singing in the back of my mind, and one day in 2014, I decided I was going to be a singer. I got a small team together and threw a concert. I sang for as long as I'd seen artists sing because I wanted to see if I could do it. It was definitely hard, but I managed to do it. I sang live and had dancers and costume changes and everything. It was exhausting, but I had the time of my life.

I decided I also wanted a music video, so I wrote a few songs and put together an album. It was a lot of work, but it wasn't hard for me because I really wanted it, and I created a team to help me do it.

When I was a kid, I always said I wanted to be a superstar. I wanted to be out there! I would see what other artists were doing—artists who had really made it, like JLo and Shakira—and they seemed really happy when they were performing. I would watch their music videos, and I wanted to be doing the same thing. It was around the time I made my own music video that I realized I was living my dream. I was filming on the beach. I would still watch my favorite artists, but I didn't have much time to watch music videos anymore because I was making them!

Even with my own career blossoming and the business growing, some people were still nervous about the path I was on. They would tell me to do things differently, or that I needed something to fall back on. It was hard to hear. I had to tell many people in my life to let me do things the way they worked for me. I listened to advice from others in the business who were doing what I wanted to do, but I tried my best not to listen to the naysayers. People try to change their formula to keep others happy, and that's when they come out with the wrong answer. I believe everyone gets to the answers in their lives a little differently. Everyone will do a puzzle a little differently. Others might finish the puzzle before I do; either way, I'd still finish.

So when my mom said things to me along the way, even when there was visible success, it didn't make sense to me at the time. Bless her heart, I know she was just looking out for me. But I knew I had to keep doing what I was happy doing. I tried the full-time job, I had many jobs before that in different industries, and I was miserable. My life was going nowhere at that point. But when I was on stage, no matter how much work there still was to do in the business, something inside me would always say, *Yes, this is right. I am meant to entertain. I'm an entertainer and an entrepreneur, whether anyone likes it or not. That's who I am. That's what it is. I'd rather work 100 hours for myself than 40 hours for someone else.*

My mom was worried about me. She would see me work so hard and tell me I needed to eat and sleep. She used to tell me she felt sorry for me and that she wanted to help me. I appreciated her love and support. But in my eyes, I was working hard, but it wasn't like I wasn't happy. I loved it. There were nights I would only get three or four hours of sleep, and it would take a toll on my body at times, but I would catch up on sleep later in the week when I could. It was just what I had to do at the time, and I felt extremely blessed to be able to do it.

I started meeting more people and getting more opportunities to perform. Everyone knew someone . . . who knew someone . . . who knew someone. I had a team that helped me do mini-tours across North America twice. I met some pretty heavy hitters in the industry. A couple of people told me they could really help me advance my career. They made some enticing offers, but there was something about going that path that didn't feel right to me.

I knew if I dropped everything and pushed for that solo career, I could have had it. I learned that it's less about talent—well, you have to have some talent, too—and more about who you meet and whether or not they want to put money behind your career. I could have gone down that path, but I didn't want to. I loved my life, and I loved Diva Diverse, and I wanted to perform and have an actual life, like an actual normal life, too. I wanted a bit of both. I knew that if I were to say yes to those offers, my life would stop being the life I knew. People would say things to me like, "You should be in LA," or, "You should be in Hollywood," or, "You should be in New York," and I used to say I didn't want that. I'd had enough of a taste of it already to know. I'd had the lights, camera, and the paparazzi. I'd done the autographs. I had a small taste of it, but it was enough for me to know it wasn't for me. I wanted my husband and I to really be in love for our entire marriage. I wanted to have a baby that I wouldn't have to hide from the media. I didn't want to have to worry about my every move showing up in a magazine. I was okay with people recognizing me from their cousin's wedding. But I didn't want the overwhelming life of a celebrity. I didn't want to have to wear a mask to go out.

I liked where I was, and I decided to stay there. I always say there are normal people, there are the celebrities, and then there's me. I liked being in between. I didn't have everyone doing everything for me all the time, and yet I was running a business I loved and had made a career of performing. And I was fine being right there.

So I just kept pressing forward.

I refocused myself on who I wanted to serve. In addition to serving my dancers and our clients, I wanted to help little kids build confidence, so I opened a not-for-profit company and threw an annual pageant called Mini Miss Diva. I was doing a lot, and things were working out, but it was tough. There were many times along the way I felt alone and hit walls. I would find myself upset a lot of the time trying to grow the business with no support. It was really just me. There was no one helping me.

One day I got so upset with how demanding it was on me to keep enough steady money flowing into the business that I was in tears. My husband came into the room and told me I had to go back to the bank because I wasn't making enough money and I was working too hard. It didn't matter how much I had on my resumé. I knew I was not going back to the bank.

I said to myself that day, *Why am I upset? No one cares that I'm crying.*

No one's going to give me money for crying, so I just need to stop this and figure it out. I needed to put my shoes on, walk out that door, and find another way.

And that's exactly what I did, every time things got tough. I just kept going and being persistent. As challenging as it was sometimes, I knew there were just certain paths I was never going to look back on. In time, the turbulence of the early days eased and the business steadied out. I developed being steadfast in my vision and what I knew was right for me and for the company. Diva Diverse was growing up.

Chapter 7

MIAMI

When you dance to your own rhythm, life taps its toes to your beat.
-TERRI GUILLEMETS

I have always had a connection with Miami. I always loved it, even before I'd been myself, just from what I'd seen on TV. I knew I really wanted to live somewhere part of the year that was like Toronto because I love Toronto, but I wanted palm trees, beaches, and the culture. I loved speaking Spanish and Latin dancing. Miami is exactly that, and I felt comfortable. So I decided to take Diva Diverse to Miami.

I didn't know what the market was like, but I wanted to try it. I first wanted to see if I could get any gigs as a belly dancer because I knew my belly dancing was really strong. I thought, if I'm able to make that mark and get my foot in the door, then I can start selling Diva Diverse.

I took a trip with my husband first. It was February, the heart of winter in Toronto. We went and scouted it out. We brought my videographer with us because I wanted him to capture our moments of discovery. I love to travel and discover new places, and I didn't want to miss a thing in Miami.

I fell in love with it. I knew immediately I could live there. It was hot, the beach was gorgeous, the people were friendly. I loved being able to speak Spanish often. Growing up speaking Filipino, I enjoyed speaking a different language. I felt like I could really be myself there. I heard Latin music in the streets everywhere. I didn't have to just play it at home, I could open my window and play it loud. I felt so at home.

We were there for a week, and when we got back, I was on fire. I told the girls we were going to go to Miami. I had no work there yet, but I had scouted out a few places we could possibly dance. These places already had regular dancers booked, and their dancers were really good. I thought if we were there together, we could all try to get work. We would be a force! I couldn't afford everyone's flight, so a few weeks later I celebrated my birthday in Toronto with everyone as a kind of farewell for a while, and at the beginning of March I packed my truck—with my husband, two dancers, my videographer, and my dog Diva and her big bed—and I drove us down to Miami in my black Audi Q5 complete with blinged out, diamond steering wheel.

We didn't have a plan for how long we were going to be there; we just knew we had to go. I still had dancers in Toronto working our Toronto contracts.

I hadn't found a place for us to live in Miami yet. I knew we would figure it out on the drive. On the way down, I spoke to a realtor who told me she had a place for us and not to worry. By the time we got to South Carolina, the place was no longer available.

We got to Jacksonville, at the very top of Florida, and still didn't have a place secured. We were five hours away from Miami, and I called the realtor again; she had nowhere for us to stay. I told her we were going to be in Miami in five hours and that she needed to find us something. I don't think she realized how dire it was until that moment. She said, "Oh my gosh, Bella, I don't know . . . uno momento . . . I'll call you back . . . I'll call you back."

I started to get a little worried.

The girls didn't know what was going on because I was trying to keep it between me and the agent. Shane heard me, though, because I was starting to freak out. He calmed me down.

Two hours before we got to Miami, she called me. She told me to meet her in a parking lot and gave me the address to put into my GPS.

"Okay." *Sigh.* I crossed my fingers.

It was the parking lot of a condo—her condo that she had just moved out of. She rented it to me for $1,800 a month, which was ridiculously expensive, but she knew I was desperate. It was my first introduction to Miami. I realized pretty quickly I had to figure out how things worked in that city if I didn't want to get ripped off all the time.

I paid that rent for three months, and then we moved into a house a little further north in a place called Aventura. The rent was a little cheaper, and the house had two pools—one at the side, and one at the back. It was *amazing.*

I covered the full rent for all of us. There was a lot of work happening in Toronto, so the company was able to cover expenses for Miami. We didn't have any work in Miami yet, so we started building. We started to slowly go out and lay the groundwork, and some clients started to sign on.

The experience was so great. I loved even just grocery shopping and cooking for the girls. I loved having rehearsal space in the house. We had to make a lot of our own costumes at that point, and I loved that as well. It was also great learning to talk to a different type of client. Miami is definitely different than Toronto when it comes to the dance scene. In Miami, most good dancers become strippers. It's actually a desired goal for dancers, and it's where they make the most money. People would say to me all the time there, "Why are you wasting your time belly dancing? You should be a stripper—you'll make two grand a night." I understood that was just how things worked there, but I would still tell them they were crazy. I could never ever do that. My grandparents instilled some pretty solid morals in me about that kind of thing. I would always explain myself to them without making them feel bad. I learned they had a completely different mentality about it. They were really humble, and very smart too. They weren't the stereotypical way people usually think strippers are. But I still couldn't do it.

I knew Diva Diverse had to compete with them, which was hard. I was a Torontonian at heart. Wearing a little costume was enough for me! So I knew we had big competition. Plus, most of the dancers in Miami had fake butts and fake boobs, and coming from Toronto, we were definitely not like that. So we got our butts in the gym every single day for two hours to try to keep up. Before long, we were in the best shape of our lives. We weren't about to go get a bunch of plastic surgery; even if we wanted to, we couldn't afford it. We needed to organically make ourselves as great as possible in order to get work.

Eventually, I got a solo residency. Residency means you perform every week at the same venue for a duration of time. It was a lot of work, and I learned why people lip-sync while they're dancing instead of singing live.

But what was Diva Diverse's niche?

I started approaching senior homes in Miami. After all, senior homes were obviously not going to hire strippers, and I found they were open to professional entertainment. It was perfect.

We ran with it. Honestly, if Diva Diverse only worked in senior homes for the rest of its existence, we would do well. We loved catering to seniors. Many of the seniors we met in Miami told us they had never had dance entertainment until we danced for them. It really became our thing. And that's how we started in Miami.

We eventually had school boards call us because they wanted dancers, and dancers who were professional and fully clothed. Word caught on, and we started getting lots of work. I knew I needed more girls in Miami and gave the girls in Toronto an opportunity to ask their parents if they could come down. Two more girls came down to join us, so there now five of us altogether working the different shows.

Diva Diverse became a lifestyle in Miami. Whenever someone hired us, they knew the dancer was going to come seasoned. They knew she would come with her fake eyelashes on and her hair beautifully curled. They knew the costumes were going to be beautiful. They knew they were going to get a professional, well-spoken dancer who was going to be great to work with, and who was going to put on an amazing show. We really started to represent the company for what it was at every show.

I started telling the girls, "This isn't a dance company—this is a *life-style*. When you wake up in the morning, know that you are a Diva Diverse member." Sure, everyone has their sad days and days when they mope around tired, wearing jogging pants, without any makeup and with their hair thrown in a bun, but I told them not to make that a daily habit. I told them if they continuously did that, they would become that person. "Put on high heels. Go to the grocery store wearing them. Put on makeup for no reason. Feel beautiful. If you want to wear a fake ponytail today, go ahead and do that. Expose yourself. Be confident in your body and your art."

When I look back at pictures of myself from that time now, some days I'd have green eyeshadow on, some days blue eyeshadow, some days orange eyeshadow . . . and did I need to be wearing makeup every day? No—but I did because I was a diva 24/7. I expressed myself. I wanted to expose my art. And that's what I told the girls. I said they didn't have to be "gangster" to match the music that was out. I told them, "Be a female. Be a diva. If you want to be all thugged-out and gangster, then Diva Diverse is not for you. It's not called Gangster Diverse. We don't wear baggy clothes. We're cool, but it's a different type of cool—not ratchet, but classy."

I told them to always look their best and be their best. I said, "When you're sixty years old and these pictures from today are developed, you're going to want to remember this. Someone's going to capture this day in a picture, and you're going to want to be proud of it."

I got some pushback at first. Sometimes the girls would still show up to their event wearing running shoes, jogging pants and a cap, with their hair in a bun, and then throw on their costume and hit the stage. I wouldn't have it. You'd better come in your high heels and your mini dress and your beautiful makeup, then change into your costume and go out that way. Because when that client comes to thank you after the performance, you are a representative of the company in your own skin. In your own person. You are a diva.

I was very transparent with them, but it was tough at times. In this generation, everything is rap music, especially in Miami, and our company just does not resonate with it. Because my husband's a DJ, I'd hear it around the house in Toronto because all the kids wanted to hear it, so I'd grown to somewhat understand it. But it wasn't my favourite. And I knew it didn't match our company at all. My dancers were these young girls, and it didn't matter what culture they were, they'd be flicking their wrists. I would just say to them, "What are you doing? Why are you acting so silly? I wanted to always make sure I was a positive influence.

Kids are kids, and when I continued to get pushback, I got smart about it: I found uniforms. I made it mandatory that the girls buy a particular brand of black dress that they would wear to their shows, as well as high heels that matched. I started documenting them if they didn't have their hair and makeup done in advance or show up in their uniforms. I knew I couldn't control what they would wear on their own time, and I learned to accept that. I could only control how they would look going to their shows. So we started there, and it worked really well.

They adopted the whole lifestyle eventually. I think it's because they started feeling good and getting more attention for their art. They started to see it was beneficial.

During the year we were there, a girl from Ecuador who danced with our company in Toronto ended up moving back to Ecuador for a few months, and then she moved to Miami. She needed work and started to manage the business for me in Miami.

So we made our mark in the city of my dreams, but it was not easy. It was not easy to do business in two cities at once. The pay was less in Miami as well, and that took a toll over time. Nonetheless, we had the time of our lives. I discovered we weren't going to make money in Miami; we were there to expand the brand, and we were there to serve a higher purpose. Ours was helping seniors get entertainment. It was a special chapter in Diva Diverse's journey.

Chapter 8

STEPPING UP

*If somebody offers you an amazing opportunity, but you are
not sure you can do it, say yes—then learn how to do it later!*
-RICHARD BRANSON

You can't build a reputation on what you are going to do.
-HENRY FORD

We lived in Miami for a year. Then it was time to come back to Toronto. I had a lot of work to do back home. Business was rolling, and I started teaching at a studio. It was a big studio, but it seemed a little shady to me. It wasn't really set up properly for dance classes. I made due for my classes, but I thought the studio was a cover-up. I thought the owner was a stripper who was washing her money through a legitimate business. She was a beautiful woman in her late forties and was making a lot of cash. I was her main teacher because I lived close by and could always teach the classes. I saw some weird stuff go on in the office at times. I was definitely suspicious.

She ended up completely disappearing. I showed up to teach a class one day, and the door was locked. There was nobody there. I called a few times and finally got the landlord on the phone. I asked if they had seen the woman who'd been renting it, and they asked me the same thing. They told me she'd been missing for a few months and hadn't been paying rent.

I had thought something weird was going on, but I didn't expect she would up and leave with no notice. I was pretty surprised, and I asked them what they were going to do with the studio.

"It's on the market."

I couldn't help it. I got really excited. "Okay. Is it a possibility I could have it?"

They didn't know me from a hole in the ground, and I expected them to say no. But they had been losing money on it for months, and I think they just wanted to get someone in there as soon as they could.

They said sure, because I was a dance teacher anyway, and I already knew the space. We made an appointment to meet at the studio. When we walked inside, we saw that the woman who disappeared had taken every-thing. It was a planned escape, and she didn't tell anyone. I was surprised she hadn't even told me.

They gave me the paperwork so fast I didn't even have a chance to talk it over with Shane. I was so excited, I signed for it. And that was it. I had my very own studio.

I put a lot of work into it and renovated it. Soon it was my dream studio. I thought it was the best studio in all of Toronto. It was on the sec-ond floor of the building, and five big panels of glass showed the Toronto skyline. We could see the CN Tower looking out the huge window. The studio itself was huge. I could comfortably teach a class with thirty people. I installed Italian leopard-print fabric over narrow benches in the long windowsill people could sit on. It had tall, twelve-foot ceilings and holes in the floor because I had portable poles that would go up for the pole class. I had the ceiling rigged for the hoop girls and the aerialist. There was a metal piece hanging from the ceiling so they could connect their hoop and hang their silk. I had contractors set it all up, and then the girls would climb a ladder to hook into it. We had taken the long, beautiful burgundy curtains with us when we left the flea market, and those hung down framing the mirrors. The burgundy and leopard print looked beautiful together. The floors were sprung for the ballerinas, and the wood was a beautiful pale shade. Every time I would walk into the studio, I would open the door and have to step up a little because of the sprung floors. I loved it because I felt like it was fitting that every time I walked into the studio, I got to step up a little bit. It was motivating and represented what the studio was for the company.

The office was off to the side of the studio. We installed a video camera system, so I had a flat screen TV on the wall in my office that showed eight different screens from different parts of the studio. I could also access the screens on my phone. I had a gigantic desk—one of those real executive desks. It was solid wood and had two massive drawers. I loved it. My two assistants had desks on each side of mine in the office. There were four big windows in the office that showed the beautiful view of Toronto as well.

To the left of my desk, there was a door that led to a massive closet of three thousand costumes (our costume inventory had grown quite a bit by that time!). It was a huge walk-in closet, big enough to be its own office. I fit everything in there: back pieces, headdresses, everything. I also managed to put a vanity in there with lights. There was a big, beautiful chandelier hanging over the vanity in the closet. I loved that chandelier because it reminded me of my first performance at my aunt and uncle's wedding when I was eight years old. Everything was custom built. There was a rack that lined the closet and rolling racks in the center. It was everything we needed.

Across the hall was Studio B and an actual vanity. Studio B was where the newer girls would practice to work their way up to being part of the prime team. Off of Studio B, there was another closet of costumes the newer girls could wear. Off the closet was another room to hang out, and then a huge vanity. Twenty girls could be in that vanity doing their makeup at the same time. I started to build showers and a bathroom for them. It was awesome.

The only downside to the studio was that there was no elevator, so we had to climb the stairs with suitcases full of costumes almost every day. But it was a minor inconvenience, and we got used to it. It was just so perfect in every other way that it didn't matter.

It was when I had that studio that I realized how far we had come. Rogers TV reached out to us and told us they wanted us on their show. I couldn't believe they'd heard about us and that they were reaching out to *us*. We were on CP24, and I had a flashback that day to when I was in my bathroom and first named the company. It was a humbling moment.

Chapter 9

TRUTH IS PROGRESS

A happy marriage is about three things: memories of togetherness,
forgiveness of mistakes, and a promise to never give up on each other.
-SURABHI SURENDRA

The business was going well. We had become an international company, I had my very own studio for the first time in my life, the media wanted us, and we were performing almost every night. But not everything can be perfect all the time. I truly believe in yin and yang, everything waxes and wanes in life; and for the first time, Shane and I hit a pretty bumpy part in the road of our marriage.

We went through some pretty crazy experiences together. In 2011, our lawyer ended up stealing $200,000 of our money. So it was tough to recuperate from, but we managed to do it. Some marriages would have divorced over losing such a big amount of money.

To be sure, Shane was really upset about it for a long while after, and I didn't blame him. But one day I said, "You know what, hon? There are problems in life. I know I've made some bad decisions in my company, and some things have gone wrong lately. But at the end of the day, we have our health, and money can always be made."

He turned to me at that moment and said, "You know, you're right. Money can always be made."

"You have your business, and I have my business, and we're young and strong. We can make that money back."

It was a tough lesson, but it brought us closer. And it wasn't the last big lesson we needed to learn together, that's for sure.

My husband never cheated on me, but I kind of did in my heart at one point. It wasn't sexual. It could have gone that way, but I knew enough to make sure it didn't. But I went through a phase where I was falling out of love with my husband, and I was being led another way. It stemmed from our differences. I was moving so fast, and the business was growing quickly. I didn't think Shane was evolving, and I started to get bored. The truth is, he was just moving at his own pace, and he needed less action to know his business was growing, but I couldn't see that at the time. I tried to encourage him to change and to try new things in his business and to take more risks.

One day after numerous heated discussions, I finally said, "I can't change you. You have to change yourself." And at that moment, I fell out of love with him. And I started falling in love with the people who I wanted my husband to be so badly.

I was around so many business owners at the time. A lot of my personal friends were entrepreneurs and owners of nightclubs, hotels, and venues. They ran big companies, or they were realtors. We spoke the same language. We were on the same level. I could say, "Let's have lunch at the TD Tower," and they wouldn't tell me it was too expensive. My husband wasn't like that, and it was frustrating me.

I used to think about my grandparents and wonder how they did it. Their marriage was so strong. My grandmother was a stubborn lady, as well as a diva. She also had her nails and hair done all the time. My grandfather was thirteen years older than her. I started asking myself, *How the heck did they stay married for so many years? And still love each other that much?* I couldn't relate in that moment.

I feared I could have a better life with another man. I started comparing other guys to him and fantasizing about the life we could have together. It was really toxic. I started hanging out with more of my guy friends and spending a lot of time with them. There was one particular friend who owned a resort who I saw the most.

One night after class, my friend came to meet me at my studio, and he kissed me. I didn't stop him. And Shane saw the whole thing. He knew I had been falling out of love with him, and he somehow figured out how to get access to my cameras at the studio.

I didn't act the way I think a normal person would act when they get caught cheating. I didn't beg him to forgive me or to stay. For some weird reason, I was glad I didn't have to hide how unhappy I was anymore. I had been telling him for a long time that he needed to change and grow, that he couldn't do the exact same thing every single day for the next ten years of his life. I said, "I don't know, maybe I'll just move out and go live with Mom." I was sorry I had hurt him, but I had been unhappy for so long and couldn't cover it up anymore.

He was so good with me. He calmed me down and said we weren't going to separate and we were going to get through it. *He* actually was the one who said he was sorry I did what I did. I wanted to sleep on the couch that night. He said no. He wanted me to sleep beside him.

I was sad at myself because I was so happy with the other guys. And I loved my husband so much. He'd never mistreated me, never hit me, always paid the bills . . . he was the best. There was nothing wrong with him. I was afraid I was going to be that girl who hurts the good guy. I didn't want to hurt him, but I also desperately needed something to change.

It was a really hard time for us. Even though on the one hand I was frustrated with Shane, on the other hand, I still knew we were going to be together forever. I knew that because my grandfather, on his deathbed, took Shane's hand in his and said in his strong Filipino accent, "You'd better take care of my granddaughter, or I'm coming for you!" Shane reassured him that he would. I remembered that moment, and I couldn't imagine giving up on my marriage.

After that, Shane became extremely motivated. He purchased a property, bought a driving school, bought a new company car . . . he manned up. He changed his world completely. We got our kitchen done. Even his wardrobe started changing.

We still argued, but we were much better. We would sometimes argue about my business. I would get really touchy when he would talk about it. I would say, "Talk about anything else, but don't tell me how to run my business." He was learning about business himself with his driving school, but we had very different approaches. He was much more conservative in his decisions, and I was always *go-go-go-go-go*. I made decisions quickly, and, in my opinion, he would take forever to make a decision. Our differences would frustrate me. I understand now that he was just looking out for me, and looking through the lens that he was familiar with, but at the time it would cause some pretty big fights.

He said something to me once that really hurt. "Why are there so many negative things around you? You're always failing."

"You know why, hon? It's because I actually try to do different things. I don't play the safe game. I will continue to fail my way to success and show people that yes, you can do it, as long as you keep trying and never give up."

It took us a while to figure out how to coordinate our differences and to see that we actually balanced each other out pretty well. Eventually we learned to see our differences as assets that helped us each become better in business. He benefited from some sparks under his butt from time to time. I learned it didn't hurt for me to take a steadier approach to things in my world.

I learned through that experience how important it is to invest in the relationship I was in, rather than looking outside it to try to solve our problems. We needed to work with what we were blessed with. We didn't agree on everything after that, but we learned how to disagree.

I went to the bridal show a few months later and saw so many young, new brides-to-be. They were so happy and giddy with their fiancés, talking about what they wanted at their weddings. As I watched them laugh and walk arm in arm, I couldn't help but think, *Do they really realize what they're about to invest in?* It's great that the fairytale has played out for them, but they won't really know what it's like until they're in it. A woman I met shortly after that, who had been married for thirty-six years, told me her trick was she treated her marriage like a job. I said, "Wow, I understand that completely." She was speaking my language.

"Treat it like a job, and one that you want to be promoted in."

I wanted to keep excelling in my marriage. I saw that if either of us were to just "do our jobs in our marriage," the other person would get bored and restless, and that's when bad things can happen. But I saw that if we both continued to excel in our positions, there would only be room for growth and room to explore new things together. People don't want to lose their actual jobs because they don't want to lose their source of income. But they don't treat their marriage like a job, because they don't think they're getting paid. But we get paid in different ways in a marriage. We started thinking about our relationship like, *Shoot, I don't want to get fired.*

Years later, after our ten-year anniversary of marriage, we were so in love that when he left the bed, I would hug his pillow just to smell his scent. So we went through our fair share of ups and downs in our marriage. But we realized our marriage was a blessing and that we were paired for each other. We continued to work on it together and not give "quitting" an option.

One day I ended up at a church reunion. As I was heading to the lady's room, I noticed

that suddenly my childhood crush was right behind me. "Falesha?"

I turned around. "Mitchell?" It was one of those movie moments.

"Wow—I can't believe you came to the reunion!"

"I couldn't miss it. We haven't seen each other in fifteen years!"

We started to catch up on the many years of life in between. "What are you doing now?"

"Well, I manage a talent agency. What do you do?"

"I manage athletes."

As we talked, we learned we still had a lot in common. His birthday was March 7 and mine was March 6. I managed dancers and he managed athletes. He had gotten married two years earlier, and I was married eight years by that point. And then he gave me a hug, and it was one of those moments of like, *Oh, this is so nice. He is still so handsome, still so tall . . .* I could have easily gotten carried away.

But then as he was walking away, I said to myself, *As handsome as you are, as good as you smell, as perfect as your career is, you know what? My husband is actually better for me. My husband makes me feel like I'm his world, he's handsome, strong, and he has broader shoulders—you're a little on the skinny side. My husband has beautiful long hair. My husband has more muscles than you.* And I was like *whoa*—I was starting to tear this guy down compared to how great my husband was! And at that moment I thought, *Okay, I think I just passed!* Because there was no guy in my life who was as handsome to me as Mitchel Friedman. It was a perfect example of a temptation from my past coming back up to see what I was going to do about it. It was like God was saying to me, "Okay, Falesha—I'm going to give this to you again. How are you going to handle it this time?" I didn't get a good result the first time around, so this time I tried something different, hoping to get a better result. And the results were that my husband was happy, nothing happened, I had no stress, and I could sleep at night . . . so much better than the alternative!

Chapter 10

THE WORST BLOW IS THE ONE YOU DON'T SEE COMING

When everything seems to be going against you, remember that the airplane takes off against the wind, not with it.
-HENRY FORD

When I was living in Miami, I had an executive director, Jenn, running our Toronto business. She handled all the emails, managed bookings, did all the admin work, paid the Toronto dancers, scheduled rehearsals, and scheduled dancers at each of the events. She was my right hand. I wouldn't have been able to expand the business internationally without her. I was extremely grateful.

While we were down there, deposits would go into the account from Toronto every time the company did a Toronto show. I noticed a few times that the deposits were not done properly. Money was taken out of the cash and given to dancers, or used for expenses, before it was deposited into the account. I knew the business and knew what numbers I should have seen in the account. I asked Jenn about it a few times, and she'd say,

"I needed to pay one of the dancers so I just took it out of the cash." I told her repeatedly that she needed to deposit all funds into the account first. Everything needed to be accounted for. But it continued to happen throughout the entire year.

She was managing my payroll because I was in Miami. She started alluding to the fact that we didn't have enough money for things. She told me once we didn't have enough money for rent. I didn't understand. How could we not have enough money for rent? We just did fifty-five shows! She would tell me things had happened that needed to be paid for. I still thought we should have had enough money. Then she started asking for additional money with no notice. Something wasn't adding up.

I was upset with how the finances were being handled throughout the year, but there wasn't a lot I could do from Miami. I knew I'd have to look at everything when I got back, and I trusted that things would be okay until then. They had to be.

Tension mounted, and I started to get a sense of urgency. I called my sister on my dad's side who had a good background in accounting. She'd told me in the past that if I ever needed her to do some work for my business, she'd be happy to help free of charge. I asked her if she might be willing to go to my office and pull up my books to make sure my finances were up to par. I knew when I got back, I was going to have to close the fourth quarter, and I was worried because we had been in the negative a lot that year. She was happy to do it.

When we got back to Toronto, my sister messaged me right away, saying there was something she needed to show me. The tone of her message was unusually abrupt and serious. "You need to come to the office, and we need to sit down and look at this."

Worried, I met her at the office right away. She had a stack of files in her arms, and when we got inside, she put them down on my desk. She started opening files and pointing to numbers. "Who is this?" she asked as she pointed to a number on the payroll table.

"Oh—that's one of our outsourced dancers."

"She's been making this amount of money?" The number did look a lot higher than the rest of payroll, but it was legit.

"Yeah, she's been working a lot of shows."

"Okay. And who's this?"

We went through a few of the larger numbers, and I explained where they all came from.

Then she got to Jenn. "So . . . why is this person expensing $11,000?"

"That's the executive director."

My sister was visibly perturbed. "And why does the executive director make more money than you?"

I was so nonchalant about it. "I guess sometimes people make more money than the CEO! She puts in a lot of work." But it got me thinking.

Then she got into the bad news. "There's a problem here. There's a lot of money I can't find. She pointed to a column. "And this money is going to strange places, and coming out of credit cards, and paying these expenses, and it's messy. None of this is clear to me."

I had two reactions to what she was saying. On the one hand, I had been concerned about the financial records for some time and wanted to get to the bottom of what was off. But at the same time, I didn't think Jenn was doing anything malicious. I assumed she was being a bit careless with making deposits properly, but I trusted her when it came to her intent. I continued to give her the benefit of the doubt.

My sister suggested I stop using the chartered accounting firm in Oshawa that Jenn had the company affiliated with, and she would go through it and analyze it herself. I brought her the files the next day.

We sat in my office together later that week.

I took a sip of a latte I had bought to ease my nerves and put the cup on the table. "What do you think is going on?"

My sister sat back in her chair, folded her arms across her chest, and looked at me. "Well, I think the paperwork doesn't lie."

"What do you mean 'the paperwork doesn't lie'?" I still didn't get it.

"Falesha, paperwork and numbers never, ever lie. That's what I learned in business. And you aren't seeing it."

"What am I not seeing? I don't get it. Tell me."

"Falesha, you're being fucked over. You need to fire her. She's stealing from the company."

It took me so long to actually believe it. Even sometimes still now I don't believe it.

My sister walked me through the numbers. She was expensing me for gas, oil changes, shopping at Nordstrom Rack and saying it was for go-go dancers, her dinners with dates, and whatever she was buying. Then when the company had little money because of all of these additional expenses, she was still putting through her payroll, leaving the company with nothing.

I still wanted to believe it could be resolved in a conversation, so I brought her in for a meeting a couple of days later.

When Jenn arrived at the office, I told her I wanted to go over some numbers with her. I asked her why she was expensing the company for gas and her oil changes. She told me that because she lived in the east part of town and the studio was in Scarborough, it took a long time to get there; it put a lot of wear and tear on her car.

I was trying to see her point of view. "Okay—and how about gas?"

Her tone got defensive. "Well, how am I supposed to get here? You said you would help me pay for gas. How am I supposed to pay for it if I don't make that much money as an executive?"

"Jenn, I mean, I don't know—I don't even expense my own gas." I was still trying to understand. "But, okay, I get it if it's a lot of driving for you. But what's all of this?" I pointed to her Miami expenses. She had come down to Miami for two weeks with another dancer to see what it was like during one of the slow months in Toronto. "Why am I expensed $600 at a grocery store in Miami? Shane and I spent $200 Canadian. You are one person. How did you spend $600?"

She said it was because of the girls.

"What were you guys buying—all organic, high premium food? Did it cost fifty dollars for one banana?"

She just kept saying it was the girls. She had excuses upon excuses.

The following week, something else came up. My sister sat me down again to show me an investment contract. At one point, during the year I was in Miami, a client wanted to invest $20,000 into Diva Diverse. Jenn had told the investor some reason why he couldn't invest the full amount into the company. What she did instead was put $8,000 into the company, and she put the other $12,000 into her credit card. Her plan was to then transfer the additional $12,000 into the company from her credit card. I didn't like it. It would have been confusing for the investor, and it was extremely unprofessional. If someone wants to invest a lump sum of money into a company, that money needs to go directly into buying shares of the company itself. Not onto someone's personal credit card.

A fraction of that $20,000 ended up in the account. But the contract confirmed $20,000 was given to Diva Diverse, to be paid an annual return of 15 percent. I think her plan was to pay the investor from her credit card every month. I just remember seeing the paperwork of $20,000, but when I checked my statements, there was no $20,000. There was $8,000, but not the money that she had forged my signature to say I was responsible for. It finally sunk in. *How is this happening?*

She brought me to court, and the judge just threw it out. It was too messy. And that was that.

While all of this was going on, she tried to take 30 percent of the corporation by saying I promised her that by a certain time, she would be a part owner of the company. It may have been a miscommunication, but I didn't make a promise to her about that. She must have been sensing impending termination. She wrote a contract saying that her mom owned 30 percent of the company, and she e-signed it.

It was a lot to take.

In hindsight, I probably should have made her a 50 percent owner of the company because I could have closed or bankrupted the company that she ran into the ground, and moved on with my trademark. It would have actually been so much cleaner that way. We wouldn't have gone to court because we would have been fifty-fifty. I should have played my cards better on that front. Then she would have been responsible for half of the debt. Instead, she was being negligent with money, and I had to take the full hit as the sole owner. She would have had less animosity toward me because she would have been doing it to herself. She would have been accountable.

She also wouldn't have been able to spread the rumors that she never got to be an owner. The thing is, it failed anyway. The rumors were just diverting attention from the real issue, which was that the finances were handled incorrectly.

I learned that I can't think with my heart in business. I have to look at numbers and think strategy. I can see a lot more clearly now. I guess that's the silver lining.

I found out around that time as well that a company had reached out by email while I was in Miami saying they were putting together an anthology of the stories of young entrepreneurs, and they wanted to interview the owner of Diva Diverse. They had seen my videos online and knew I was from Toronto. They wanted to feature my story.

Jenn didn't tell me about it and sent in her own story instead. I realized it when I got back and saw they had sent her a draft of her story back to her. She had written a story of her life as a dancer and being part of Diva Diverse, and they put it into the book.

I always try to give people the benefit of the doubt. I tried to convince myself she must have misinterpreted what they were asking. But when I looked through the emails, there was no way she could have not known what she was doing. There were so many emails. She had lots of opportunities to tell me they wanted to interview me, and she didn't. Not once. She was the executive director, and she wanted the opportunity.

I ended up firing her in January of 2015. We hugged each other and we were kind of crying about it. I just said that it was honestly what it had to come down to. I said we had a great ride, but that she had made some bad decisions. I admitted that no one's perfect and I had also made some bad decisions. But I said we had to leave everything as it was with the pros and the cons, and part ways.

Chapter 11

FALLOUT

*I'm stronger because I had to be, I'm smarter because
of my mistakes, happier because of the sadness I've
knows, and now wiser because I've learned.*
-CURIANO.COM

It turned out that was just the beginning. Then came the fallout among the team. When I was in Miami, she had gotten a lot closer with the girls. When all of this went down, she spread rumors among the team, and I lost a lot of my dancers. A few of them left and started their own dance companies to become my competition. Jenn took a lot of our clients and customers. People would call her phone while I was in Miami, and she went ahead and made contracts with them after she left. That was another silly thing I allowed. I should have always insisted on all client calls going through the business phone.

Things had already started to go sideways with my Toronto dancers when I was in Miami. I used to have meetings with them at the beginning or end of rehearsal to make sure everyone was on the same page and give them pep talks. But there's no question not being in Toronto for a year took a toll on the relationships with my dancers.

Before I went to Miami, my Toronto dancers and I were friends. I discovered when I first went to Miami that I had to be more of a business-woman with them because I wasn't there in person anymore. I was Skyping into their rehearsals. I think some of them got envious, or at the very least annoyed, thinking, *Who does this lady think she is, coming in on a Skype call in rehearsals telling us what to do?* From the perspective of a business owner, I was thinking, *Yes, but you're dancing in my studio that's very expensive. I'm giving you money to do gigs so you can make money. These are my three- or four-thousand-dollar costumes sitting in that big closet.* I needed to keep a tight ship while I was away and couldn't be everyone's best friend. I couldn't play Barbie anymore. I would thank them for their attention and get down to business. If one of the managers told me something happened at an event, I'd take a "Guys, let's fix this" approach. It was friendly, but to the point. We all had work to get back to.

But I could tell I was losing their loyalty. I think some of them resented that I was in Miami with four dancers at one point, and they were dancing in Toronto. I didn't know how to resolve that. I couldn't afford to bring everyone to Miami, and we needed dancers to fill the gigs in Toronto. I hoped they would continue to do what they were doing for the love of what they were doing, but I think some of them were too young not to let it get to them.

It showed especially on one particular night when we had ten shows booked. In our rehearsal meeting the night before, I asked the girls to send me pictures of themselves in costume at the shows they were doing so we could use them for marketing. I asked them each for one so we would have one from each of the shows. Everyone said yes in the meeting.

Sunday came. I got no pictures. Sunday night came. I still got no pictures.

As they were finishing rehearsal that night, I called in on Skype. I said I was really disappointed. They were all standing in a circle while the manager held up the phone, looking at me blankly as if to ask me what was wrong. I said, "I didn't get one picture. There are fifteen of you. I saw online that you guys were taking duck-faced selfies on IG, but none of you sent me the one thing I asked for. What am I going to put out for social media? It's Monday tomorrow."

They were quiet. One girl spoke up. "Um, yeah. I really don't appreciate being talked to like this."

I just said, "What do you mean? I asked you guys politely, on Friday, to take one picture."

They started siding with the girl who had voiced herself and started saying in a kind of messy chorus of excuses, "We had ten shows, and it's very hard to take a picture while we're working."

"It doesn't matter if it's not easy; you can still find a way. And how do you squeeze in time for a selfie of you doing duck face when you can't get a picture that's part of your job?" I basically reminded them they were getting paid for their shows and that these kinds of things weren't optional. It was part of their job, and if they didn't want to do it, they should let me know.

I never got mad. For me to lose my temper, they knew I was upset. It was a mistake that I was so lenient with them in the first place. It's a lot harder to soften your leadership style after setting firm rules, boundaries, and expectations than it is to do it the other way around. They were so used to doing whatever they wanted, and when I started pressing them for more, they resented it.

More and more grumbling started among the girls. As I was growing into a better and more mature businesswoman, I was changing from the way I used to be with them. It was a tough transition. The girls started looking at me differently. I started hearing rumors in the dance community that the girls were saying things like, "Falesha thinks our company is so great," and "Falesha thinks she's the best," and I remember it was so strange to me. I didn't understand it. Why would someone start a company and not want it to be the best? Isn't it natural for someone to give their all to something that they think is the best? People don't start companies saying, "I want this to be a mediocre company," or, "I'm going to be at the bottom." No—they strive for success. It started to drive a wedge between myself and the dancers.

It didn't help that when we all got back from Miami, the four girls who had been able to join us down there came back with dance videos, bragging about it. I think it worsened any animosity toward me the girls in Toronto already had. Then all of the legal stuff went down with Jenn, and it was the last straw.

Before I knew it, I lost about twelve girls in the space of a few months. In business terms, it happened pretty much overnight. They all quit.

The business was definitely going through growing pains. I started to realize everyone has an expiry date. And for those girls, it was just their time to move on. They did what they had come to do with the company, and it was time. We made awesome videos, we made lots of promo material, we did great things together, but they didn't see the long-term vision. They let the issues that had come up get to them. Truth be told, the company did take a lot in a short period of time. I didn't have the experience of running a company from two cities, and I could have made some better decisions. It was a stress test, and we failed.

I learned a lot, to say the least, in those months after coming back to Toronto. I was different after that. First of all, I realized I had two brands and that they overlapped: The Diva Diverse Brand and the Falesha Raquel brand. I started separating them and working on them independently. I also started looking at the different roles I had in the company and figuring out how to better separate them. I was a dancer, and I was the owner and CEO. I had to act differently when I was in those different roles, and I couldn't just be so free and easy about everything anymore. I realized that the messiness in the business in the prior year stemmed from things I wasn't doing as well as I should have been. I started to put integrity into my roles within the company.

It was such a hard time for me that it took me a year to cry. I was so in shock about everything for so long that I didn't cry for a year. And then one day it just all came out.

In the months to follow, I had to rebuild loyalty among the Toronto team. I had to practice making the shift from being everyone's friend to being the owner and holding everyone accountable for doing their work. It was a tough transition to make. I got a lot of pushback.

I remembered back to a conversation I'd had with another dance company owner who I really looked up to at the time. She had started renting my studio once a week, and we would talk when we'd see each other. Her company was very successful—they were even on Desperate Housewives of Toronto the year I'd met her. She said something to me once that really made me think: "Falesha, do all of your dancers get along? And do they all respect you?"

At that point, I'd never had any drama in my company. "Yeah, of course."

"That's amazing. They never fight?"

"Never." The company was so blessed at that point. I really didn't understand how blessed we were. But she was my senior, and she'd been in the game longer than me. I wanted to know what she was trying to tell me. "Why?"

She chuckled a bit. "Oh—you're lucky. My girls give me attitude *all the time*, and there's always some kind of drama going on. But whatever, we're still doing our thing."

Did I ever think back to that conversation when I lost all my girls.

I found out later one of her girls betrayed her too, in the same kind of scenario. Mine was a little worse because it was financial, but she had someone steal costumes and clients from her as well. Then I understood why she said that to me when she did. She was probably wondering if I had gone through it yet because she was much older than me. When she was renting my studio, Diva Diverse was on top. Everyone in Toronto wanted Diva Diverse dancers or wanted to be a Diva Diverse dancer. But I learned through her experience, and mine, that not every dance company can be on top all the time. It's kind of like entertainment. You have an artist like Drake who's on top, and then Beyoncé, and then Nicki Minaj. One artist can't be on top forever. It's the same in the dance world. Another company will always come up and take your place, and then you have to come out with new choreography and new costumes. That's our hit.

So Diva Diverse fell out of top position in Toronto, and I accepted it. We weren't the talk of the town anymore. But we had already made a name for ourselves, so it was just a matter of time. We needed to rebuild.

Shortly after that, I didn't renew my lease and closed the studio. I would have had to renew for another four years, and I didn't want to carry the expense after everything that had happened. The company was still financially crippled, and we had lost a huge portion of our talent.

Chapter 12

NEW STEPS

Do not be embarrassed by your failures.
Learn from them and start again.
-RICHARD BRANSON

It probably sounds silly, but it was through this difficult time I realized the company had made it. I remembered one day back to when I had first started the business and said to my mom that I wanted the CRA knocking at my door to know who I was. And I had just gone through getting sued, which I won! My mom told me I was ridiculous.

I said, "Think about it, Mom: People know who we are. I was sued. It wasn't fun, but it means we're something worth fighting to get money from. The fact that this company has money because it's done well means we've made it."

It became a turning point for me. I wasn't afraid of legal issues or anything in the business world anymore. The experience not only gave me a thicker skin—it showed me the company had reached a new level.

It also made me a better business owner and manager. When my girls weren't taking their jobs seriously, I had started to put pressure on them. But I was still a dancer myself in the company. It was confusing for me, and for them, at times. I knew I needed to learn how to start doing a better job of giving people what they needed in each of the capacities I needed to fulfill.

I had a lot of rebuilding to do, and I realized I had to change.

My mom always tells me my heart is so big I always get hurt. She said to me once I was lucky I was married because if I was out dating, I'd be depressed all the time. I think she's probably right. I love really hard. For all these years in the business, I wanted to give everything I could to my dancers. I'd invite them to my house and make them food and tell them to take whatever they needed. But it didn't work. They stopped taking it seriously and would call me last minute to say, "Oh Fee, can you just do this show? I can't do it." They'd let me down. They wouldn't follow through on things I would ask them to do. And when I started to get upset with them for not taking their job seriously, they left.

I knew with this new beginning in the company, I had to figure out when I need to be who with them. I needed to create a clear boundary between business and friendship, but I couldn't do it without rebuilding my relationships with the girls I had left.

In rehearsals, I dropped the business owner role and was a little friendlier with my girls again, but made sure I maintained all of the rules and standards. I started being friendly and firm at the same time. I started to relate to them again and talked about topics they were interested in. They weren't necessarily things I cared about, but I cared about rebuilding a connection with them.

I started going to rehearsals and changing my high heels at the front door of the studio before I would walk in. I knew I had to have a little posture with them, to make sure they took the job seriously and to make sure there was respect for the rules, but I wanted them to be comfortable with me.

I watched how the girls responded and tweaked and tried things to make our relationships better. I would try something new with the girls, and they'd hate me. I'd change it up, and they'd love me. I'd just keep trying and trying and trying. It wasn't that I was faking it; it was that I was learning what people needed. And every particular group of girls needed something a little bit different.

I started focusing more on mentoring the girls, both individually and as a group. A lot of girls that came into the business at the age they were at were really lost. Some of them had come from broken homes, just like I had. I would see in rehearsals that they lacked confidence. I'd start teaching them their belly dance routine, and they'd say, "I'll never be able to do that!" The words "I'll never" would just irk me, and they'd say it so much! So I started really focusing on their development as confident women, and I'd coach them. I started giving them guiding words and uplifting motivational speeches throughout rehearsals and whenever I'd see them.

But I couldn't always be a coach. I'd have to go back and forth between different personas. If I stayed in one role too much, they'd get annoyed. So I learned and practiced and, in time, I started to rebuild the relationships with my dancers. And I'll certainly never be finished learning this. Working with people is an art, and I'll always be looking for new ways to connect with and inspire my dancers.

I didn't have my own studio anymore, so I started renting studio space for us to rehearse. I knew I at least needed to have my own office, so I rented a small office in Yorkville to run the business out of. I would meet clients there and spent whole days on the phone booking shows. In time, my assistant took over the day work at the office. Again, I was firm about the rules and what needed to get done, but I let her know that as long as she got it all done, she could set her own hours. Sometimes she'd be at the office all day. Sometimes I'd be at the office, and she'd Skype in with me. I didn't want to be taken advantage of, but I didn't want to be down her throat. I tried to be the boss my boss at the bank wasn't. I was so intimidated by him. He would make a comment about everything about me. One time I went into work with green nails. They weren't a grotesque green, but a nice summer green with a little bit of glitter on them. He looked at my nails and said, "Really, Falesha? Green nails?"

I said, "Excuse me, Jeff, does your wife not wear nail polish?"

"She would never wear green!"

"Well, I'm not your wife!"

"Look, I'm just saying . . ."

And this was my boss. It really bothered me that he was always so condescending. I knew I didn't want to be like that with my assistants. As long as they looked professional, I'd let them wear funky clothes to work all the time. They'd wear whatever made them happy. I'm an artist myself, so I thought it was awesome. I love when people can express themselves.

I knew that working with someone you actually like is so much easier than working with someone you're trying to stand for a full day. Sometimes my assistants would be at the office for ten hours. They loved their jobs and wouldn't even realize how much time had gone by. I'd have to say to them, jokingly, "Can you leave? I'm still paying you! Go home!" We had a good thing going.

I learned in those days of rebirth how important it was to keep my business and marriage separate. I'd be the businesswoman with clients, the mentor with my dancers, the cool-but-firm boss with my assistants . . . and when I'd get home, I loved that I could just fully be myself with Shane. Having any of the titles I had didn't change who I was at heart. And I could be that person fully with my husband. He had the driving school, so we'd come home at the end of the day and talk about our businesses. We'd talk about all we went through with the lawyer. We'd talk about what happened with Jenn and how things were going since then. At the end of the day, literally, we were each other's rock, each other's foundation. We had been through so much together, and we were still by each other's side. I was so grateful for him.

I had developed a thick skin in the business, but underneath it all, I was still me. Shane would see my vulnerable side. I'm actually a really emotional person. If you make me laugh hard enough, I'll cry. But I'd learned in hard situations to curb my emotions and just say, "Okay—how are we going to figure this out?" I'd feel like if I were crying in that moment, I was weak in that moment, and I couldn't be weak. In the business, it I was either going to sink or swim. I didn't have time to cry. I was even told a few times that I needed to work on my emotional side. When one of my dancers would come to me with a problem to do with their boyfriend, for example, and they'd be crying, I would empathize and give them advice on it, but I wouldn't cry with them. Sometimes I'd actually stop for a moment and say to myself, *Wait, should I be crying? This person is having a breakdown, and I'm fine . . . I'm so emotional—why am I not crying?* My friends even started saying to me that it was hard for them to come to me about things they were dealing with because I handled things so differently than a normal person. I used to get that all the time.

I think it was good for them that I didn't feed into the heaviness of what they were dealing with. I didn't want to feed the drama. I had empathy for how they felt, but when something was wrong, I'd pick their brain. "Tell me, what is going on? How did this happen?" I wanted to know so I could help them.

They'd say, "No, it's okay. I'll tell you another day," and try to change the subject.

I thought at times they were embarrassed to share what was wrong with me because they'd break down and I wouldn't. I'd be empathetic about it, and then say, "Okay—how are we going to get through this?" I always wanted to help them find a solution. I thought, *Crying is not going to get us anywhere.* "How are we going to fix this together? I'm here for you as a friend. What are we going to do?" As emotional as I was underneath it all, I didn't want to just sit there talking about how the world was ending. "Do you need a vacation? Let's look online and book one. Do you need ice cream and cheesecake? Okay, let's go to the grocery store." As I grew to be less emotional in the business and with my friends, I became more solution-oriented with everyone.

But it was when I'd come home at night, after all was said and done for the day, that I could be vulnerable with Shane. And it was while I was rebuilding the company that I really grew to appreciate this aspect of our relationship so much more. Who he gave me space to be at home helped me go back out there every day and be better for everyone I was serving. He got all of me, and I loved him for it.

Chapter 13

GOING GLOBAL

We had already brought the company to Miami, and I wanted to bring Diva Diverse to other parts of the world. With Toronto going strong again, and with a better foundation, it was time to expand.

Sometimes we don't realize we've made it until we look back on things. We may think we know the significance of something in the moment, but we really don't know it until later.

I started traveling here and there and performing in other parts of the world. I would go to resorts and showcase my belly dancing because I knew it was really strong. The two places I started were Mexico and the Dominican Republic.

Someone decided to showcase my international dancing and made a video of me called "Belly Dancing with Falesha, International Belly Dancer." I didn't really consider myself an international belly dancer until I saw that video. I mean, we had already brought the company to Miami, but I still didn't really consider myself an international dancer. But in that moment, I realized, *Wow, I'm performing on stages in different countries. I* would sign autographs for people after the shows. I was a star to them and in my own little world.

I really got it when I watched playbacks and videos people would take of me and post. *I'm your star. I'm on your flyer. You guys paid $100 a ticket to get into the venue and see me.*

One of the times I was in the Dominican Republic, I performed on the same stage Ashanti had performed on earlier that day. I stopped and actually realized that one day in the moment. I said to myself, *These people are like me. They're entertainers, and they go around performing to make a living.*

That is when I realized there's no such thing as competition. Coming up in the business, I always thought I needed to figure out a way to be the best. I needed to become the best belly dancer around so people would continue to hire me over other dancers. It was a mentality of scarcity, as if there wasn't enough business to go around for everyone.

But there's no need to compete once you really find yourself. I used to be so offended if somebody tried to step into my world or copy a routine. I used to think, *Oh, who's she? What does she think she's doing?* I was that person. But when I was dancing on international stages, I realized there actually is no competition. For anyone. We are all our own artists, and we all add our own unique flare to our art. I realized that the best belly dancers in the world are still not Falesha Raquel. We still have our own steps, our own way, our own finesse. And we all have our own fans. There's so much work out there, all over the world. And if I was good, and I worked very hard at becoming confident in my talent, then I knew I'd get booked, regardless of who else was on the scene. I realized I was my own brand. As I got to know myself on those stages, I realized competition is an illusion.

There was a time I was worried about not getting enough work. I was always worried someone was going to take my job. I can't believe it took me that long to figure out that no one could replace me. No one can replace any artist. Who do you know right now doing exactly what Shakira's doing? Only Shakira. Once when I was in the Dominican, I was talking to the other dancers at the resort, and they were calling me Shakira. I said, "No, no, I'm not Shakira. I'm Falesha."

There are so many belly dancers and singers, and it doesn't matter. I did a gig back in Toronto where I danced for the owner of Mattamy Homes. I danced to Despacito because it was the new, hot song. I made it unique.

There are dancers who do things that I don't do. There are steps and moves I have practiced and perfected that I've never seen any other belly dancer do. We're all different.

I realized it also applied to Diva Diverse. After so many of my girls left, a bunch of dance companies popped up. I realized when I was dancing internationally that it was fine. There were clients for all of us. My girls and I can respect another school and their dancers. Everyone is great at what they're great at. A client may want our style based on our costumes or musicality, or they may want another company's dancers based on their ethnic background or dance strengths. It's all fine. There's enough business for everyone.

Rather than incessantly comparing Diva Diverse to other dance companies around us anymore, I focused instead on how I could continue to bring the business to the next level. And the next thing I did was buy a house.

I always wanted a large portfolio of investment properties, but my husband and I never saw eye to eye on that topic. Especially because I wanted things done yesterday. I actually bought the house without him knowing! I don't purposely get myself in trouble trying to be mischievous or to cause trouble—it's just I have my own personal desires and goals, and most of them are pretty big. My family is from the Philippines, and we had nothing growing up. I don't know why I seek the things I do. But I am always looking for the next level for the business and for Shane and me.

My goal before I turned thirty was to own an apartment building. Instead of a Trump Tower, it was going to be a Falesha Raquel Tower! I knew thirty was approaching, and I wasn't even close to that yet, so I wanted to own another property. I said to Shane one night over dinner, "Babe, what do you think about us buying a house? Just as an investment . . . the market's really good right now . . . I really think we should do it." I was doing really well at that point in my career, and he was very busy with his work. It seemed like the perfect time to me.

He conservatively said that we had already lost $200,000 with the lawyer and that we shouldn't be doing anything crazy. I said, "Are we going to wait until I'm forty years old to have an investment property? Because I should have at least had a condo by now!" The subject was dropped.

I didn't have a lot of money, but for some reason I knew I would find it. I knew it would happen.

One afternoon, I was buying an outfit for a performance, and the owner, a friendly gentleman, happened to be working. As I was cashing out, he handed me his wife's card and told me she was a realtor. He said I should get in touch with her if I was ever looking to buy. I couldn't believe it. I asked if she would work with someone in the arts. I didn't work a nine-to-five, so I wasn't sure if I'd be approved. He said she specialized in working with business owners. "Wonderful." I was pumped.

I called her the next day. "Hi, Luna, my name is Falesha. I got your number from your husband while I was buying a dress at his store. Would you mind showing me some houses?"

She started showing me properties right away. I fell in love with the eighth property she showed me. It was a corner unit, 1500-square-foot, four-bedroom, three-bathroom house located in the heart of Scarborough. It wasn't too expensive, and I knew I could carry the mortgage. I wasn't sure if I'd get approved but wanted to try.

Luna told me I couldn't be approved without having someone else on title with me. We needed to up my income or add someone else's credit. She said she could have approved me for a condo, but not a house.

My mom and Shane did not enter into my mind as options because I already knew they weren't really into the idea, so I automatically started thinking of people I thought might say yes. Who was I going to find?

I approached my assistant to cosign with an offer of 1 percent equity. I was excited about the idea of having a house I might be able to offer to dancers from other parts of the world who wanted to come to Canada. I already knew dancers from Mexico, the Dominican, and Ecuador. The dancers in third world countries are exceptional and better than a lot of dancers in the Western world. They work harder because here we have everything handed to us. I wanted to bring the Dominican girls, the Cubans and Brazilians, African girls. And I didn't want to pretend to be a Hawaiian dancer; I wanted to bring a dancer from Hawaii and give our clients authentic shows. I envisioned having ten girls in Canada at a time.

After all, Diva Diverse stands for culture and diversity. I couldn't wait to be able to offer them a place to stay. We talked about all the different possibilities. She said, "Falesha, you're my boss. I'll do anything for you." I had a cosigner.

I came up with the down payment and got the house.

I had local renters at first. One night six months later, I said to Shane, "Hon, can you get into the car? I have something I want to show you." I called my tenants and let them know I was coming over to do a quick drop in. No one was home, and they said to go right in.

We pulled up in the driveway, and I opened the door. "Ta dah!" I said with my arms outstretched.

Shane looked baffled. "Whose house is this? Why are we here?"

"This is our investment property!" I said with a big smile.

"What do you mean our investment property?"

"I bought this house for us!"

He was upset . . . but happy . . . and confused . . . and when I get nervous, I start talking really fast. I explained why I did it for us and for our future kids, and eventually he came around. In time, he was actually really grateful that we owned another property.

I didn't start on my plan of bringing girls to Canada right away because there was so much to focus on in Toronto. It would have been too much to juggle alone at that point.

I ended up telling my mom about it one day. She was still renting and was scared to buy. My tenants were still in university, and I was having trouble with them. I had to fix a hole in the wall that they punched when they were drunk. It wasn't ideal. And most importantly, I wanted to offer my mom a nice place to live. I asked her if she wanted to move into the house.

She was ecstatic. She moved in right away. I'll never forget the moment I was able to give my mom a home.

I opened my diary up months later and read that one of my goals I had written down years earlier had been to buy a house for my mom. I had completely forgotten that I had written that. I was pretty grateful it had come true.

Things were going so well, and I felt like I had really made it. I was an international belly dancer, the business was thriving in Toronto again, and I was able to take care of the people I loved.

We're so rich in Canada; it's incredible. We have first dibs on technology and on everything, really. When I was in the Dominican, the women there were asking me what kind of makeup I was wearing. Even if I had told them, how would they be able to get it? It's not like there are MAC stores anywhere. And hair products . . . it's no big deal in Canada when someone asks about that.

"What hair product do you use?"

"Oh, I use Pantene Pro-V."

Great—you know you can go to the store and get the same thing. You can afford a seven-dollar bottle of conditioner.

In the Dominican Republic, it's like a dream. The women there would say to me, "I hope one day I can get that Pantene Pro-V," or, "Are you going to leave a bottle for me?" Maybe they'd never get that opportunity again.

I also didn't want women to have to worry about pads or tampons. Every time I go, I bring lots of both and give them to all of the women. We take it so lightly. We just go to the store and buy pads for the time of month.

I wanted to open a store there. I saw they needed a bridge. They needed someone who cared about them to source things from Canada to give them a little taste of our life continuously and for them to have products to meet their basic needs. Not like a one-time opportunity, but continuously.

I had always dreamed of having my own little store. I didn't want to pay commercial space rent in Canada because I knew it would cost me $5,000 a month to lease a little storefront on Yonge Street. In the Dominican, Falesha's store would cost me $150 Canadian a month, and I'd be helping the women there. It would be like a little taste of Canada. I haven't committed to it yet, but it's a dream I have for the future. I envision putting together a little group and going down for six months to get things set up. In the meantime, I try to bring as much as I can down to the women when I travel. I want to share as much as I can with them.

We can't help the whole world, but we can help small communities.

I had been afraid to share things, no matter what it was, because I was afraid of competition. I was always afraid someone was going to surpass me. I think in general people are scared to share because they're intimidated of the other person getting better. But after spending time in places in the world that had so little, I grew a deep yearning for contribution.

Once when I was in Cuba, I brought a whole plate of pizza backstage for the dancers before we went on stage because I hated being hungry. I needed something, so I brought pizza for all of us. They told me it was so good and that they could never afford it themselves. "Do you know how long it would take to get us all this pizza?" I couldn't believe it. It was such a small thing for me to pay for, and it made such a huge difference for them.

I wanted to help the women there. I wanted to help them believe in themselves. I realized, too, that we carve ourselves out in the world when we share what we know. I wanted what I had learned in business to help someone else. It's always better to share things with others.

When I travel now, I find myself wanting to bring the dancers to Canada. Some countries are harder to do that in than others—for example, Cuba. But for the most part, it wouldn't be too difficult. I imagine sending girls from Toronto to other parts of the world to have them experience that culture, then bringing girls from those countries up here to give them a Canadian life for three months at a time. The basement is open in my mom's house. The girls could make money here, and go back home rich. So far, I've connected with someone in immigration in the Dominican and now have to do some research in Canada on how to make this possible.

I want to help these women become divas in their own way. I want to help them bring confidence and resources back into their own countries. When I think about their families and communities, I want to make that kind of impact. I want to bring divas into a diverse world, ready to contribute everywhere.

I think to myself sometimes, if we succeeded in Miami and America, imagine what we could do on a little island.

Chapter 14

OUR ART IS OUR GIFT

What I know is that if you do work that you love,
and the work fulfills you, the rest will come.
-OPRAH WINFREY

It's been a long and amazing journey. Diva Diverse has come to a point where it's in a steady, mellow chapter. I don't know exactly what I'm going to do next with the business. I'm enjoying watching my dancers grow up. I always say to myself, *Maybe the next big Diva Diverse dancer is still really young right now, and she's just growing up.* It's amazing to be at a point where I can observe the business running without needing so much of my own time and energy.

There's one aspect of my life that most people don't know about me. Shane and I have been open to getting pregnant since we got married. It hadn't happened yet, and it was probably for the best because of how much was happening in both of our businesses. But there would be times we would really focus on trying, and nothing would happen. After a while, we'd kind of give up and get busy with life again. It didn't seem like much of an issue for many years. We just thought it was part of the plan. But when I turned thirty, I started to get a little worried. Not to mention, Shane is nine years older than me. It was getting late.

We did all kinds of tests, and the results came back normal. My eggs were fine. Shane was fine. I started going to a fertility clinic. Every time I'd go, I'd see the women sitting in the clinic all depressed and I'd try to talk to them to cheer them up. It was a depressing place. It's really tough as a woman not being able to get pregnant.

It's not easy for me either. And when people look at my life now, they don't know I'm going through this. I wasn't even sure for a long time if I was going to put this in the book. But I think it's important because it's become a big part of my life and my journey.

I've been applying the things I've learned in business to this situation. There were always obstacles that would act as barriers to my dreams and goals. I'm certainly not new to things not being easy. And how did I always get from point A to point B? Sometimes I went around. Sometimes I went under. Sometimes I went over. Sometimes I went through. But I always got there.

People ask me all the time when we're going to have kids. I've realized now that, actually, I don't know. We don't know. I sat down with my doctor the other day and said to her, "I know Shane's healthy. I know I'm healthy. I know everything is fine. It's just a matter of time." Because everything's perfect: I eat healthy, I work out . . . I'm following all the rules. This experience has helped me see how much I've changed over the years. Falesha three years ago would not have accepted the fact that I'm having trouble getting pregnant. I probably would have really lost my cool and forced payments, or found a surrogate, to make it happen. Now I know it's not right to try to force it, especially when we're talking about something as sacred as new life. What's meant to be will be. We can wait for the right timing.

I've learned that when I think I know, I really don't. There is always so much to learn. I listened to one of Oprah's lectures recently. She said in the talk, "If your purpose is to inspire, stop fighting it." It really hit me. It was so clear. *That's it.* Really, when I think back to everything I've done, I've wanted to inspire. I want to inspire customers to appreciate the arts and hire talent. I want to inspire my girls to become their best. I want to inspire women all over the world to be confident and offer their gifts to their communities and those around them. I want to inspire people to follow their dreams and monetize their talents. I even thought about all of the girls who have come to my dance company who have been inspired enough to work against me and create their own dance companies. Not exactly what I had in mind in the first place, and they may not have gone about it in a positive way, but they were inspired to start something of their own.

I hope to also inspire a more compassionate world in general. So many women see me or see others and think we have perfect lives. If I could only tell you how many times I've been to clinics this month and how many times I've had to give blood . . . you never know what people are dealing with behind the scenes. I've had to do so many things to try to get pregnant. I've had to put on so many smiles when all I've wanted to do is cry.

But I will keep going. We will keep going. We will continue to trust. And we know everything will work out the right way, in the right time.

I don't think I would be able to have this perspective without having learned everything I learned as the owner of Diva Diverse. I now see that God gave me that business to teach me. He wanted me to grow and to learn how to become a better person. And when I started getting distracted, He pulled me back on track.

You know, sometimes when people see me in the mall or somewhere on the street, they say, "Oh, hey! You're the dancer girl, right?" I know they only see me on stage, but they don't realize that there is so much more to my life than being a dancer. I put years of blood, sweat, and tears into the company as the owner. I almost lost everything, then had to fight to build the company back up. I'm building up women and communities in foreign countries. I'm a coach and mentor. I'm a wife. I hope to soon be a mother. *What do you mean I'm just a dancer?*

No one is just a dancer. No one is just an artist. Our art is our passion, our gift. And our lives are full expressions of what it looks like to do what it takes to express that gift. We are never just our art—our art is the gift we were given to help us become who we were meant to be.

PART TWO

Find Your Path

I wrote this book to share my story with you, but not for the sake of telling you about my life. I wrote it to hopefully inspire you to take action on your dreams in your own life, and to give you strength and support along the way when you do start taking steps forward.

Maybe you have already started pursuing your dream of making a living from your art. If so, congratulations on making that decision. Use this next section as fuel to propel you forward and keep you moving into greater growth and discovery.

If you haven't made the decision to really go for it yet, and you are just beginning to look at the idea of monetizing your talents, you are in the perfect place. Enjoy the inquiry and use this section to explore what it could be like for you if you decided to move forward.

These are the four things that helped me the most on my own journey: *Determination*, *Intelligence*, *Value*, and *Attitude*. Together, they spell *DIVA*. This is not an accident! I discovered that, at the end of the day, all I was learning was meant to support my life's mission with the talents I was given. Without these four qualities, I would not have achieved the success I did, despite the many setbacks and obstacles I experienced.

So remember: When it seems tough, this is when you are developing the determination, intelligence, value, and attitude to support your life's mission and realize your dreams!

Chapter 15

DETERMINATION

*You never know when you'll find success. You
just have to keep striving for it.*
-PITBULL

*You should never view your challenges as a disadvantage. Instead,
it's important for you to understand that your experience facing and
overcoming adversity is actually one of your biggest advantages.*
-MICHELLE OBAMA

Success is not a destination, and there are always going to be challenges. New things you hadn't thought of before are always going to come up. It's not like once you put all of these pieces together, all of a sudden everything is just going to be easy and perfect. And the process is not linear. As a business owner, you are always in a process of growth, discovery, and adapting to change.

Despite your best-made plans, things are going to surprise you. How quickly can you adapt? When you keep your focus on the value you provide people (your clients, your audience, your team), it is easier to adapt to changing circumstances. When things are challenging, rise to the occasion. You'll have to do things before you think you're ready. Try these tips and reflections to support you in being able to adapt to whatever you need to along the way.

We all know how important it is to be determined to succeed, and you now know from my story that determination was the cornerstone of my own success with Diva Diverse. It's one thing to know something, and it's another thing entirely to actually *follow through* with it! Here are some ways to work and live with determination.

Shift your mindset from setbacks to successes.

I learned through many difficult situations that no matter how bad things got, I had to shift my perspective from what I saw as a setback to how I could use it to fuel my success. Remember when Shane and I lost $200,000? That was one of the hardest times in the business and in our marriage. And we had to push ourselves to see that, despite such a huge financial loss, we still had our health and each other. We also had our talents and our businesses, and instead of lamenting over the loss, we chose to instead focus on how we could make back the money. It was probably one of the hardest times we've experienced, but our determination carried us through.

My first shift was to recognize that the problems I had in the business were a reminder that I actually *had* a business! I wrote in my journal when I was young that I wanted to be a very successful businesswoman. When problems come, I don't go back and say I don't want it anymore! The culmination of our dreams will come with both the good and the bad, so we need to be ready to deal with both. I didn't realize that success was going to come with so many challenges, but I knew I couldn't give up on it. You have to be careful with what you really want in life because it's going to come with all that it comes with, and it will come with trials and tribulations ready to teach you how to conquer them.

When you experience a problem or a setback, consider that what you are interpreting as a setback might actually be a learning moment on the way to your success. In time, you will be able to look back on the situation and say to yourself, *Wow, I'm actually glad that happened. I didn't know it at the time, but it was the best thing for me.* You can probably think now of a time or two that this has happened to you already. Hindsight is twenty-twenty, and everything makes sense in time. So when you're in the middle of what seems like a catastrophe, be grateful for the hidden benefits you don't yet see.

There's always a way to shift your perspective.

Let's Get Real:
When has a challenging situation turned into a learning moment for you?

Sink or swim, but keep going.

When you step up and try something in your business for the first time, it's going to be sink or swim. But here's the thing: It's actually less important whether you sink or swim, and more important that you have the work ethic to keep going, or to get back up and try again. If you swim, don't let the win make you lazy. Don't take your foot off the gas. Don't think you have something handled and stop working for it. If you sink, don't let yourself get discouraged. Accept the loss and get back up and keep going.

You're going to have to develop a discipline and a thick skin in order to create longevity. If you don't have both, you'd better work at developing them! Without discipline, you will be overly swayed by the circumstances in your business, and your results won't be consistent. Without a thick skin—the ability to hold your ground and to hear things and to not take them personally—you'll find yourself stressed out often. It can be catty and toxic in any industry, and this industry is no different. It's not that you have to *be* the bitch, it's that you have to know how to *deal with* the bitches. When you're not blown about by every wind, you can develop a cadence and a consistency that will carry you ever forward toward greater success.

Let's Get Real:
What do you think could help you stay consistent and determined in work ethic, emotional state, and attitude through the inevitable ups and downs in business?

The people in your life can be your support.

When you are feeling the pressure to quit, lean on the ones who love you to infuse you with new determination. Everyone you know is in your life for a reason. There were many times that I'd come home, exhausted, and fall into Shane's arms. He was my rock for many years—and still is! My mom pushed me to keep doing whatever I needed to do to make the business successful. Her doubts, although from a loving intent, actually motivated me to succeed. My ballet teacher telling me I couldn't make a career as a belly dancer motivated me to prove that it could be done. My friends helped me, and still do, to see myself objectively—they always give me raw, honest (and often unsolicited!) feedback, and it helps me to see what I need to work on. My dancers consistently show me how to be a better leader. Because of them, I am constantly challenged to grow and improve as a person, mentor, coach, and business owner. My audience shows me, ruthlessly and in real time, what I am doing well as a performer and what I need to improve on. I am grateful for every single one of these people. I wouldn't be who I am, or where I am, without them.

Let's Get Real:
Who are the people in your life who can help fuel your determination? How do they contribute to you, whether they are aware of it or not?

If at first you don't succeed . . .

Success is not easy, and finding your place in this world is not easy. But there does come a time when, if you have been barking up a tree with no results for long enough, it's time to try something else.

When I was a ballerina, I didn't have a body like a ballerina. I couldn't do an over-split. I hated pirouettes. I hated having to do grand plies. I realized at one point that I was really unhappy, comparing myself to people who were much better than me. I didn't sense it was my place. Then I found belly dance. I found something else in my craft I was much better suited for. Walking away from ballet was not the end of the world.

Now I have ballerinas looking at me saying, "You're such a good belly dancer; I really wish I could move like that!" And when I was in school, I was wishing I could move like them!

There's so much in this world that you can do with your talents, and there are many ways to get there. Don't get stuck in a cocoon thinking there's only one way.

As you now know from reading my story, I've been shut down a lot. I also tried many things before I set my heart on being my own boss. When I first started making money, I worked in retail. Then I worked in food service. I bought my car doing that, but all of these things weren't making me happy. So I got my car sales license. I became Ontario's youngest female to have the highest car sales in the company. Then I got my mortgage license and started closing mortgages. I tried all of these things because I wanted to give myself an opportunity to see if I really liked it.

Success is related to how much you enjoy what you're doing, and how great of a fit you are for what you're doing. When you find your true calling, it's easier to really succeed at it because your heart will be in it. Give it your all with everything you try, but if it's not working after a long enough while, try something different.

Let's Get Real:
Is there something you have not been succeeding at in your business that you could put more effort into nurturing to success?
Have you been trying something longer than you should without seeing any results? What other things could you try instead?

Get used to failing!

Instead of letting your hardships and failures
discourage or exhaust you, let them inspire you.
Let them make you even hungrier to succeed.
-MICHELLE OBAMA

If there's anything that Shane can make me cry about, it's when he says things like, "You've failed so many times. When are you going to actually learn? How can you say you're a successful businesswoman when you fail all the time?" I know he means well, and he says these things out of concern for me, but they come from the fact that we have different styles in business. I take much bigger risks than he does. We complement each other well in that regard. But it still hurts to hear it sometimes!

I don't try to cover up my failures. They have made me who I am! People come to me now for advice on things I learned the hard way. I hear things from friends and family like, "How should I do my taxes?" and "Remember that time you got sued? How can I prevent the same thing from happening to me?" I've been at rock bottom. I give people advice on things because I was at the bottom of them and learned how to overcome them. I had to figure out how to go about setting up my company to make it a successful company in the eyes of the CRA. I had to deal with the IRS in Miami. I had to work with lawyers. I was audited. Yes, I failed at a lot of things along the way, but I had to in order to be where I am now.

I'm not afraid to fail anymore. Now, when I'm going through a challenge, I actually say, "God, you're awesome. Thank you so much. I know I'm going to get through this, thanks to you." Although I admit sometimes I'll ask Him to go easy on His next task for me!

No matter what, failure is an opportunity to get to a higher level.

Let's Get Real:
When have you turned a failure into a success?

What are you afraid of failing at? What would be possible if you let go of that fear and knew you could adapt if you needed to?

Your troubles should fuel your determination.

When you are trying to get a business off the ground, you need to know that troubles will come. Expect those troubles and have the determination to work through them. When I got taken to court over not making my executive a part owner of the company, I was glad to have that problem—because it meant Diva Diverse was established enough to be worth suing! This might sound funny. But when you think about it, everyone has problems.

As artists, especially once we take the step to move forward with a business plan, we can get so caught up in the problems that come up in running the business that we can forget how amazing it is to be able to do what we do. What are you good at? What is your artistic zone of genius? If you have a natural talent, that is truly a gift. Our art is a deep source of fulfillment for us and a source of contribution for others.

There will always be problems in life. The question is, what kind of problems do you want to have? If you can reach a point where you are grateful to have the natural issues associated with running a business as an artist, you know you're in a good place—you can use those problems as fuel to keep fighting and improving!

Let's Get Real:
What talents do you have naturally?
What problems associated with your art can you anticipate and imagine yourself working through?

Anything's possible with hard work.

You can make anything possible with hard work. Success did not come easy to me. I worked my butt off to get where I am. I've been through lots of ups and downs—many times over!

People looking at my life often think that I just have things handed to me, but I know the truth. Without my fierce determination to succeed, I never would have gotten to where I am today. Success depends on our measure of determination. We have to do the right thing with the gifts we are given. We have to put in the work and the discipline. Nothing of any worth comes without hard work and determination. If you believe that and put it into practice each and every day of your life and in your business, you *will* be successful. Period.

Let's Get Real:
What area of your business do you work the hardest? Do you see the benefits of that now?

Chapter 16

INTELLIGENCE

Your world is only as small as you make it.
-GABRIELLE UNION

Life is a series of choices—make smart ones.

Your life is determined by the choices you make. Where you are now is, in part, a result of the choices you've made in the past. As author, speaker, and trainer John C. Maxwell says, "Life is a matter of choices, and every choice you make makes you."[1] Indeed, "Choices are the hinges of destiny," echoes poet Edwin Markham.[2] What you decide to do each day influences your future. This is good news! It means you have tremendous impact on the direction of your life and business based on the choices you make.

It is also imperative, then, to use intelligence with every choice you make. Every time you say yes to something, you are saying no to something else. Have you been saying yes to things you don't really want to fill your time doing, and saying no to your passions and talents?

Once you have a business, always think through your decisions as president. Don't ever feel pressured to make a decision about your business quickly. If someone asks you about something, if the answer doesn't come to you quickly, or you feel a bit uncomfortable about it, go home and evaluate the situation. Sleep on it. Be analytical. One decision you make in your business can impact many people—your team, your family, your clients, etc. And your choices can really impact your reputation. Take your time, and choose wisely!

Let's get real:
What choices have you made in your past that have helped you get to where you are today?
What choices can you make now that will help you move closer to the ability to spend more time sharing your art?

Success is about habits.

If you keep habits that are conducive to success, you are much more likely to be successful. Habits are things you do over and over until they become routine. Everything you do is a habit, whether you are aware of it or not. If you press the snooze button often, that's a habit. If you have a tendency to not follow up with clients right away or give same-day service, that's a habit. If you put off work you know you need to do, that's a habit. If you're sloppy about the finances in your business, that's a habit. We tend to think of habits as things like flossing our teeth or going to the gym. While those are also habits, we are acting out of habit every moment of the day.

If you are serious about success, you'll need to take an inventory of your habits. Start with asking yourself what habits you need to keep in order to be the best you can in the business and as a performer. For example, as a dancer, I need to get the gym every day because I need to keep my body in shape and increase my endurance. I have to eat the right things to keep my skin looking good. I need to drink enough water. I need to pack meals when I have long days of rehearsal. I have a full morning routine to get my mindset right for the day. I have a nighttime routine to clear my mind for a good, rejuvenating sleep.

I've also learned to say no to bad habits. I learned after my divine meeting never to eat an edible again. It's just not for me. When my brother's friends are over now, and they ask me if I want some, I say "No way—but I can make you guys food!"

Let's get real:
We just explored choices. Choices, when repeated, become habits. What habits would help you improve your art and business?
What habits do you have right now that you need to give up in order to drive toward excellence in your business?

Find the resources you need.

There is a book out there for *everything*. Especially today, with the surge in entrepreneurship, coaching, and mentoring in the last ten years, and with access to a plethora of different resources online, you can find support for whatever you need help with in your business, every step of the way. There are books and experts that focus on every aspect of running a business, from writing a business plan, to accounting, to hiring, to leadership, to monetizing your specific art. If you're feeling stuck at any point along the way, find the resources you need and get the most you can from them.

Let's get real:
What aspect of monetizing your art do you need support with?
What resources can you think of to help you?

Master your craft.

When you're at a restaurant and you order something to eat, after a certain amount of time, it comes to your table. Then you have to figure out how you're going to eat it. You have to cut it into pieces and actually do something with it. You don't just sit there and look at it. You put the milk and sugar in your tea, and you stir it until it's drinking temperature. There's work that comes with it, especially for it to taste good!

Running a business is no different. Many people want to have a business showcasing their art for a long time, but then once it comes, they don't do anything with it, or they don't know what to do with it, and they don't find out.

There is work involved in creating success. Yes, you can want things and ask for them, but then when God gives them to you, it's your free will in terms of what you actually do with them. Some people get an opportunity and decide they don't really feel like doing the work that is required. They thought it was going to be easier. They say, "Never mind—I'm not going to do it after all." Then they ask for something else, and then when that thing comes in, they decide they don't feel like doing that either. After a few cycles of this, they decide, *Nothing's working out for me,* and they go into victim mode and feel like a failure. This is a sabotage mechanism that erects barriers to success.

When you pray for something and it comes in, it actually takes something from you. Your dreams don't come with automatic success. They come as opportunities, and it is your job to see and accept the opportunity, then to be willing to do what it takes to make something of it.

The only way you can master something is to put time and work into it. Sticking with something long enough is the only way to get there. If you are sure of your art, you probably know what I mean. When you know your talent and you know what you're passionate about, it's easy to be 100 percent committed to being a dancer, singer, guitar player, painter, sculptor, or whatever gift you've been given. It's all you want to do, and you thrive on working at it and getting better. Just the sheer passion for your talent drives you to do it enough to continue to improve. Unless you have a parallel passion for entrepreneurship, it's significantly more difficult to stay as committed to mastering running a business. If you've been trying to book a certain type of show (weddings or private events, for example), and you're not getting success right away, it can be tempting to say, "It's not working out," or, "This is too much work," and give up. It's an illusion that anything will just take off automatically and not require a bit of elbow grease. It is going to require a degree of effort, long enough, to get your business rolling in any direction.

So stick with it. As you learned previously, there comes a time when, if you've been working at something for long enough and not getting results, you have to adapt and try something else; but don't change directions *until you've actually put some work in.* Do not interpret hard work as a sign that what you're doing is not right for you. Even the perfect path requires effort.

When you do find success in a certain direction—you know your audience, and you've started to master a particular niche in your business—continue to master your company's unique contribution. Keep driving up the quality of your costumes. Continue to drive toward greater degrees of performance mastery. Drive toward higher degrees of excellence in choreography. If you're a singer, get yourself a loop pedal to improve engagement and excitement at your shows. Do not stop. The more effort you put into mastering both your art and business, the greater returns you will get.

Finally, always work toward excellence, but not perfection. It is a waste of time and energy to expect or strive for perfection in your art or your business. You don't have to be perfect—just keep continuing to grow.

Let's get real:
What do you need to revisit in your business and put more effort into to cause success?
What can you do to take your art to the next level?

Know the truth about money.

Everyone in this world wants to make money. We live in a world that revolves around the dollar. It's understandable that money is important, on some level, to everyone.

That being said, there is a point where a drive for money becomes unhealthy, and actually destructive. Many make decisions in their business or career based on money. They say, "I think I should do this because there's a lot of money in it," or, "I want this future because it will make me a lot of money." While money can (and should) be a factor in your decision-making process, money in and of itself is not going to make you happy; it's the progression of working toward achieving your goal that makes you happy. Money is just the icing on the cake.

When I perform for one particular wealthy client for fifteen minutes of an act, he pays me $500. But the $500 doesn't make me happy. Yes, $500 is nice, and I need it to pay for my gas and a few necessities, but it's the being on stage and doing what I love that means the most to me.

Another thing to keep in mind about money is, the more you make, the more expenses you will have. Sure, there is always room to play with your equations and margins, but it's generally true that your income and expenses averages out to be about the same ratio no matter how much money you're making. Do you remember the song, "Mo' Money, Mo' Problems"? There's something to it. Of course, this also depends on your lifestyle choices, but my point is simply, don't assume that just because you're *making* more money that you're going to actually *have* more money.

There was a point when I realized money wasn't an issue for me anymore. I didn't really think about it. If I went to a restaurant or shopping, I didn't worry about how much something was. I wasn't worrying about the things I used to worry about. But then I started realizing that money also wasn't making me happy. I had money, but what I was doing with it wasn't fulfilling.

When you live with intelligence, you will understand the wisdom of allowing money to be a useful tool and resource but not an ultimate goal. Yes, having money opens doors for your business, makes some aspects of life easier, and lessens your anxiety, but it is not the end goal. When you do what you love, people will see it and be drawn to you, and the money will come.

Let's get real:
Where have you been wasting or hoarding money?

How can you use the money to create more value for the people around you?

A healthy mindset supports your intelligence.

The nuts and bolts of running a business are one thing—and at the end of the day, your mindset is the most important. There's no sense in learning about how to set up a business if you think it's going to fail anyway! It is your responsibility to keep a good, healthy mindset. While personal support is also important, get yourself the emotional support you need *outside* of your immediate circle of family and friends. I always recommend to entrepreneurs that they hire a coach for an objective, third-party perspective. I wrote this book to support you with this aspect of running a business and to encourage you to increase your belief about being able to get to where you want to go! I also have a coaching program available to help you see your blind spots in different situations and through the ups and downs in business. If this is something you are interested in looking into, check out my website *www.falesharaquel.com*. There are also many other coaching programs and resources available to help you support your mindset.

I often find that journaling supports a healthy mind. Try writing regularly to express your concerns and worries on paper. You might find that as you write and empty out the clutter from your mind, solutions start to come to you!

Let's get real:
What would help you support your mindset?
Is there anything you'd like to commit to starting?

You are the common denominator.

If you want to succeed, you need to be responsible for everything that happens in your business. When I discovered my executive assistant had been stealing money from the company—whether she had meant to do it maliciously or not—I learned that I hadn't been present enough in my business. I didn't catch it early enough. Even when I thought something might be up, I let things slide and I was irresponsible.

Don't blame others for failures. When something goes wrong, look for what you could have done differently. I learned quickly after the fallout from my executive assistant leaving that I was responsible for becoming a better leader to my team if I didn't want to keep losing people. It was not their fault things weren't working—it was up to me.

I am now fully present in my business. There is no cheque cut in my company that I don't sign. I don't care how big the business gets or if I have multiple partners—cheques will always cross my desk for me to personally sign.

As your business grows, and as you need support, you'll need to outsource things, but you still need to be responsible for every single thing that happens in your business.

Let's get real:
Have you been blaming someone else for something not working out in your business? If so, what is it, and how can you be responsible for changing it?
What would help you stay present in your business as it grows?
What are the aspects of your business that you need to be responsible for, and doing yourself, as the business owner?

I've heard it said that a smart person makes a mistake, learns from it, and never does it again, but a *wise* person finds a smart person and learns from her how to avoid the mistake altogether. That's what I want for you as you read this book. I want you to learn what I've learned, apply the wisdom I've fought hard to gain, and avoid the setbacks I experienced. You can become an intelligent *and* wise individual who makes smart choices, weeds out the bad habits, and chooses a healthy mindset each and every day.

Chapter 17

VALUE

*Surround yourself with people who see
your value and remind you of it.*
-JENNIFER LOPEZ

I've met many talented people to tell me they "used to" be a singer or dancer, but that they aren't any more because they need to pay their bills. I get it—I was there. I know what it takes to live and make ends meet as an artist. It's not easy, and sometimes you have to spend less time on your art than you'd like. *But that doesn't mean you are not still an artist.* If you are a singer, you were born a signer, and you will die a singer. If you are a dancer, you were born a dancer, and you will die a dancer. That's true whether you're actually sharing your art or not. Who you are, at your core, doesn't change, regardless of what you're doing or not doing.

You have incredible value as an artist, and you can share that value with the world! Follow these tips and complete these reflections to help you shine.

Share your gift now.

It's so tempting for us as artists to say, "I don't want to put myself out there yet because I'm not ready, I'm not big enough, I'm not good enough yet, I don't have enough people on my team yet." We stop ourselves because we think we're not where we need to be.

Let me tell you: There will *always* be someone who your talent is perfect for. No degree of talent or skill ever goes to waste. If you're not sure if you're ready for a main stage in a public venue, fine—start performing at schools. Get family together and share your art with people who you know will appreciate it. Keep getting yourself out there, and you will naturally become better in front of an audience, and gradually work your way up to bigger and bigger performances. Don't let the "I'm not ready" excuse stop you from sharing your natural gift, now.

Let's get real:
Have you dissuaded yourself from performing somewhere because you think you're not "ready?"
Is this actually true? If so, where could you perform instead?
Have you been telling yourself you're not ready to start a business from your art? What do you feel about this now? What small first step could you take to resist excuses?

Keep your boundaries.

One of my younger cousins told my mom and I the other day that she was considering stripping. She's twenty years old. I said to her, "Breanne, you know Mom's worked really hard all our lives to give us what we have, right? You realize that it's not okay to do that, right?"

She said, "Yeah, but they make a lot of money . . . and then I can have a car like yours . . . and I want to travel more."

I told her that everything I have, I worked my butt off for it—*without* being in that game. I told her I'd never done drugs, or sold drugs, or stripped, or been an escort. I told her that was dirty money.

All she said was, "But why not? You'd make so much money!"

"Listen, hon. Would you like to know how many times they tried to recruit me while I was living in Miami? Sure, I could make two grand or five grand a night . . . but you know who I think about whenever I'm about to do something wrong? My grandfather, with his Filipino-looking face with his glasses. He's right there telling me, in our language, to think about it. He reminds me of our morals. Our family doesn't do things like that."

It's what has stopped me from smoking—I've never tried a cigarette in my entire life. I don't look down on people who smoke, but my grand-father was a heavy smoker, and he didn't want me to pick up the habit. I once actually *tried* to try a cigarette when I was younger with my sweet cousin Maddie. We went to light it, and the lighter just wouldn't light, and then it started raining. I clearly wasn't supposed to try smoking. He didn't want me to.

My cousin was raised in modern culture, and was never as close with my grandparents. So I tried to help her see what I was talking about an-other way. She has a younger sister, Rina, who looks up to her. "Bre, next time you think about stripping, and you picture yourself on that pole half-naked, do something for me. Picture Rina's face. Think about her sit-ting in a chair and watching you saying, 'What are you doing? I want to be like you when I'm older.' Would you want your little sister to be like you?"

"Ew! Why would I want that for my sister?" She started tearing up.

"Then, picture this. You're in a bathroom. You've been in the industry for five years now. You need to get a little high because you need to get on stage. So what do you do? You take some cocaine. Now your boss comes in and you're getting raped."

She freaked out.

"Exactly. That would be your movie. And that's just the beginning of the movie. Now let's look at how your movie ends. Are you going to go to jail? Are you going to end up pregnant with some customer's baby? Are you going to end up dead?"

Tears. She saw the consequences if she made that choice.

"Or are you going to decide not to do it in the first place? How do you want your movie to end?"

"I can't believe I actually wanted to do it."

"Yeah. Money is great, but money is not everything. Do something you love that is more important than the money, and don't turn your back on yourself for some fast cash."

Identify your own personal boundaries in business and do whatever it takes to guard them. No amount of money will be worth doing something that doesn't lead to your ultimate good.

It's important to also keep boundaries with your clients. I had a client once who charged his banquet hall customers $100 to watch me belly dance. He didn't give me a percentage of that fee—he kept the entire $100 for his company. It was when I was just starting out, and I did it for the love of dancing and having the opportunity to perform. I also got to keep tips the audience gave me directly. One night, he texted me without notice and said, "See you tonight." Prior to that, I would drop anything I was doing that day to get there, but I knew I needed to set some boundaries. I sent him a text back saying, "I saw your text, and I'm sorry, but I can't be there tonight. I have commitments. I'm going to be at a dance workshop. Thanks for thinking of me, but I'm not able to make it on such short notice."

It can be the hardest thing in life, when you own your own business, to say no. You might be afraid of being replaced by that client, or you might just hate the feeling of guilt that can come with letting someone down. But you have to set boundaries for what kinds of jobs you will take and under what circumstances, and stick to that policy, so you don't burn yourself out. Saying no to something that doesn't work for you or the business might be uncomfortable, but it is *immensely* better for the business, and you and your entire team, and ultimately your clients, in the long run.

Let's get real:
Is there something you did in the past just for the money that you didn't think you should do? How did it go?

What boundaries can you see to set now? What will you never do just for the money?

Ignore the naysayers.

Most people are motivated by fear, and when you step out in your business endeavors, there will be people who will try to discourage you. Whenever one of those people tells you not to do something—and it will happen, if it hasn't already—ask yourself if they have ever done what you're trying to do. If they haven't, then they are not qualified to give you advice on it. They simply don't know what they don't know.

You are also a completely different soul than somebody else. No one is going to have the exact same desires and thoughts as you. If someone doesn't see the value in what you're doing, it doesn't necessarily mean you should stop. The people in your life, most often, mean well—thank them for their input and for caring enough about you to worry about you! But remember you are on your own path.

Some people just generally don't have an optimistic view of life. It's usually because someone in their past was pessimistic toward things they were doing, and they listened to them, and then became pessimistic themselves. And sometimes people say random things in the spur of the moment, and they don't realize the impact they have. One day when I was sixteen years old, I was singing in the shower. My mom came in and said, "Can you stop?! You can't even sing!" I cried in the shower until I got out. I brought it up three years later, and she cried. She said, "I didn't mean that. I was just having a bad day and you were singing at the top of your lungs, and you were in the shower for like half an hour." For those three years, I had let it bother me. It was something so little to her, but it actually stuck with me. I eventually got past it because I realized people say things they don't mean when they're upset.

Now my mom brags about my music all the time and tells her friends her daughter is such a great singer (thanks, Mom!).

So remember that other people's opinions of you are actually just coming from wherever they are at the time, and they might have nothing to do with you. It might not even technically be their opinion—what they're saying might just be giving you a window into where they're coming from that day.

Finally, no matter how good you are, you can't please everyone. Some people are not going to like your style. You have to understand that. The flipside of this is that, no matter what, you will have an audience that loves what you do. I cringe at some of the crazy heavy metal bands out there, but they make millions of dollars because there are lots of people who love that kind of music. Every single artist has an audience. If your art isn't being appreciated somewhere, go and find your audience.

Let's get real:
Think back to a time you got negative feedback from someone. Could it be that what they said had more to do with where they were at, than with you? What do you see now about this?

Keep your word.

A huge part of living your values in your business—and in all aspects of your life—is keeping your word. When you say something, make sure you follow through on it. This goes for all things, big or small. If you tell a client you will get back to them later that day with a booking date, make sure you get back to them that day. If you promise your team you pay them by a certain date, make sure to pay them by that date.

No one is perfect at this, and it can be difficult to remember everything we commit to. When you make a promise, write it down so you can make sure you remember to follow through. And if you can't follow through on something you promised, make sure to acknowledge what you said, and give a new alternative that you can fulfill on. Or, if you have to, retract the promise, accepting the consequences of doing so. It might take time to rebuild trust in that relationship, but honoring your word to that person will be the first step.

This is especially important and requires some skill and practice at balancing out the different areas of your life. If you're married, make sure your business does not undermine the promises you've made your partner in any way. And don't allow anyone you meet in your business to distract you from where your heart is meant to be. Especially if your spouse isn't an entrepreneur, this can be a temptation. Think back to what happened to me. If you ever find yourself starting to fall for someone else, and you're not as attracted to your spouse anymore, it doesn't mean that you don't love them or that you're not supposed to be with them anymore. This is a trap, and one that will cause distraction if you act on your feelings. If this happens to you, you're just distracted with something shiny. Your old toy doesn't look as attractive against your shiny toy. But you have to shake it off and break out of it. Your old toy has been with you since you were young. It's broken and you've fixed it. You've taken it everywhere with you. If you trade in your old toy that you love for a new shiny toy, what happens if it breaks and you can't fix it? What happens if it gets old and you lose parts of it and never find them again? But you know your old toy that's perfect for you? It became your old toy *because* it's perfect for you. Don't get distracted with something new and fancy.

If you have feelings for someone, those feelings are there for a reason. They're trying to tell you something about the relationship that you're in. Rather than jumping ship and trying to find an answer in a new direction, ask yourself what those feelings are trying to tell you about where you are now. If you give up on a marriage, or a relationship, you're just going to have the same issue you're dealing with come up with somebody else. You'll keep getting the opportunity to learn a lesson over and over until you're willing to actually look at it and learn from it. Work on it where you are, and you'll find freedom and fulfillment you never thought possible.

Let's get real:

None of us are perfect. Is there something in your past you've made a promise about and not followed through? Is there something you need to clean up with someone?

What are some ways you can balance the different areas of your life so you can honor your word with everyone?

Is there somewhere you're not putting your most important relationships first? What can you do to change things around so you can keep your priorities first?

Let others contribute to you.

This might sound counterintuitive, but it's an act of generosity to let others contribute to you. Courtney Westlake, storyteller, wife and mother says:

> *People truly want to help, and by rejecting their offers and desire to aid you in a time of need, you are doing a huge disservice to not only yourself, but to them as well. Accepting help is actually giving others the gift of being able to take action and show love to you when they might otherwise feel helpless.*[3]

I have learned over the years to let my friends, especially, contribute to me. It keeps our relationships strong. Truly, I don't know what I'd do without them. I get so busy sometimes, and to me it's just normal until someone calls me out on it. My friends have pulled me aside and told me I seem really tired at times. It takes them saying it for me to actually realize it! I'll take it in. "Oh—I guess I am kind of tired. That's probably the reason my body hurts so much lately."

They'll say things to me like, "The reason you're feeling sick today is because last week you went outside in your belly dance costume in the heart of winter."

"Oh—right. I did do that. I should stop doing that!"

I thank God for my friends. I have one friend in particular who really tells me things straight. She watches my life that way and pulls me back on track if I need it. She's like my feedback loop. I've talked a lot about determination in this book, but don't be so determined you don't let others help you!

Let's get real:
How can you be more generous in letting your friends and people in your life contribute to you?

Step up when you need to!

There are going to be times when you don't want to adapt to a new situation. It's much more comfortable to back away from doing something you've never done before than to step up to the plate. But it's the only way you'll grow. No matter how uncomfortable it is, walk into that bank and open that bank account. Don't worry too much or overthink things to the point where you talk yourself out of them. You will rise to the occasion if you give yourself the chance to. In fact, you *have* to in order to really make it.

As a business owner, you're going to be going through a lot of "firsts": first time interviewing candidates for your team, first time hiring someone, first time filing a corporate tax return, first time losing an employee, first time getting negative feedback, first time reaching a revenue level in your business. Every time you experience a first, you're going to have to grow. Don't wait until you grow first . . . it doesn't work that way! You have to step up first and have the courage to try. Then, in actually doing it, you figure it out.

Let's get real:
What have you been avoiding in your business that you see you need to step up to take on?

Don't get stuck in the past.

It can be tempting to worry about what might happen in the future because of things that happened in the past. It's a much better use of time to focus on what's in store and on how you can improve your future with the choices you make now. Think of your past only as much as you glance in the rearview mirror—a quick moment from time to time just to see what's there. Learn from what you see about the past, then adapt. But you should be spending most of your time looking out your front windshield at where you're going.

If this happens to you, if you get stuck in the past, thinking about it more will not help you move on. Tell yourself quickly that whatever happened, happened, it's all good; you're moving forward, and you're better for it. Your value is determined by who you are, not just what you've done.

Let's get real:
Have you been fixated on something that happened in the past or that makes you worry about the future?
What can you extract from that past event/situation that can help you in your business now?
How can you refocus on where you're going instead of thinking about the past?

Always focus on providing value.

People have called me a diva my whole life. But what does that actually mean? Is it because I wear makeup and heels? Is it because I walk with confidence? To me, a diva means a feminine force that is confident in herself and successful—and, most importantly, *that focuses on helping others.* Divas, at least by my definition, are not high maintenance or selfish; they contribute good to those around them. They want to help others.

I have days where I have tea or wine with my ladies, and other times I have someone crying on my shoulder and my job is to help them see that everything is going to be fine. I turn into whatever they need in that moment to support them.

My job as a business owner is also to provide value for everyone on my team. There are people working in my company who don't want to own their own businesses, but they are happy to be part of Diva Diverse because they are aligned with it. One of my dancers said to me once, "I don't know what I would do if I wasn't dancing here and making a salary with you." I realized in that moment how important it was for me to get up every morning to do what I do. Because if I didn't, the people on my team wouldn't be able to pay their rent. I realized the clothes they were wearing were bought with the money I was able to pay them. I freaked out! I was so grateful to be able to provide work for them.

Remember the time I started being harsh with my girls, and they all started to leave? It was a lesson to me in how important it was to provide emotional and mentorship support to my team as well. It's never enough just to pay someone. Money can't buy loyalty. I needed to also make them feel valued. I learned that if my dancers loved the way I treated them, and loved the vision of the company, and loved everything about our brand, they would work hard to help push us to the top. I believe we don't get to where we want to get in life alone. While I ran my business myself, and took my own initiative to learn what I needed to learn along the way, every person who came into my life along the way, and every single dancer on my team, helped the company get to where it is now. If you contribute to your team, they will contribute to your business and vision.

Finally, when I'm on stage, and there are the cameras, lights, and music, I give my audience a show. I am always looking for more ways to give my clients value.

If you ever have an issue with a client, look for how you can over-deliver to turn the situation around. Small gestures go a long way.

Think of this as circles inside each other: The one in the center is the value you provide your company, which enables your company to provide value for your clients and audience, which then enables your company to provide value for communities, and eventually the world.

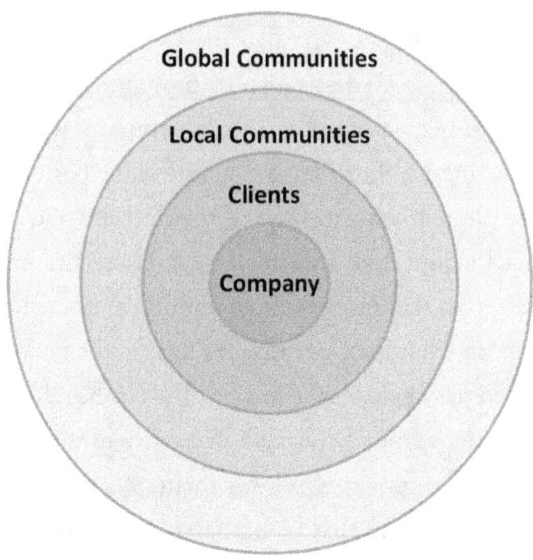

I was sitting in a bar with a couple of gentlemen one night, and they asked me where I was from. I told them Toronto, and they told me they were from Moncton, New Brunswick. We got to talking about business, and they suggested I fly out to Moncton to consider expanding the dance business out there. They said they didn't get a lot of entertainment out there and opened my eyes to new possibilities, even in Canada.

I ended up working a contract in Saskatchewan for one year. I flew out every fourth weekend. I belly danced in a stadium for the Indian community. I got connected with the gig through a couple who used to take me on Bollywood cruises to perform.

Every time I go to the Dominican Republic now, I look for ways I can help the women there. What else am I going to do while I'm here? Life can't just be work, for the sake of work. I'm always looking for ways I can help other people or expand the business or increase the value of what we do for others. That will never stop. There will always be more value to give and more people to entertain and more differences to make.

Always look for how you can give more value and more service to more people. That will always lead you in the right direction. Your gifts were given to you so you could provide value for somebody else. Always look for where you can provide that value.

Let's get real:
What value does your business provide the different people it touches?
Can you see ways your business can provide more value to others?

When you know your value, and set your focus on providing value through your work and business, everything else will fall into place. Share your gifts, set boundaries that underscore your worth, and always be on the lookout for opportunities that add value to what you're already doing. Embrace your value and your worth, right down to your core, and there is nothing that can stop you!

Chapter 18

ATTITUDE

The greatest discovery of all time is that a person can change their future by merely changing their attitude.
-OPRAH WINFREY

In both my personal life and in business, I've always done things kind of backward. I got married at twenty-two and then decided to start a business. That's far less common these days than doing it the other way around. When I registered my business, people told me to chill out and to start getting clients first. I sketched out a business plan after I had basically put together my business model by experience. Most people never understood me because I did it all backward, according to them. But that's how I needed to do things—it was the method that worked for me, and I discovered that by getting out there and doing things, then adjusting along the way. Once you are in action, you'll find that your own unique method will emerge.

Let's get real:
Is there something you do differently from others you know because it's the method that you've learned works for you?
How can you not be swayed by others' opinions of what you have learned works in your business?

Find your audience.

You are a unique artist, and you will always have your own fans and unique following. There is no better way to contribute than to find the people who appreciate your art the most.

How can you identify your audience? Well, first of all, they are obviously people who love what you do and want to be a part of it. You will find it easy to inspire your audience, *and your audience will inspire you.* You'll find yourself wanting to improve for them. You'll find yourself wondering what they're into and follow how their tastes are changing, and you'll want to deliver according to their wants and likes (that is, while remaining true to yourself and your unique style). Your audience will drive you forward. You'll find that they will contribute to you as much, if not more, than you contribute to them!

Let's get real:
Who is your audience?
How do you inspire them, and how do they inspire you?

Bring people with you.

So what do you do when you have money and fame? Then what? I'll tell you at the beginning: There's so much more to this journey.

People say it's boring to be on top, that it's boring to be wealthy because you have no one to share it with and no one who really understands you. So if you know it's going to be lonely at the top, why not take a few people you love with you?

After the situation I had in 2014 with my executive assistant, I asked God for a very solid inner circle. I didn't care if it was small; I just wanted the relationships to be real and long-lasting. I wanted a small group of friends who I could walk shoulder to shoulder with. At the end of the day, the most important things in life are the people around you, and the experiences you share together. Bring people with you along your journey to make it fulfilling and worthwhile!

Let's get real:
Who are you blessed to have in your inner circle? How do you contribute to each other in unique and important ways? How do they enrich your life?

> *We are what we repeatedly do. Excellence,*
> *therefore, is not an act, but a habit.*
> —ARISTOTLE

As an artist and business owner, it is your job to keep the standard high, no matter what—regardless of what people around you are saying or doing, regardless of what other companies in your space are doing, and regardless of what anybody on your team is doing. Keep your eye on where you're going, be sure of what you want, stick with it, keep growing, and *always* drive toward excellence.

There is no competition.

When you really know yourself—like really know that your particular talents are unique and unlike anyone else's—you will start to see that you actually have no competition. No one can be better at you than you.

Envy is a toxic and draining emotion. It's bad for the soul! Try not to watch social media too much. Work on your own craft and just put it out there. The more you watch other people, the more likely you are to start comparing yourself and bringing yourself down. It can really mess you up. It's one thing to watch others to learn from them and improve your own skills. But when you look up other companies in your space too much— beyond a quick glance to see what others are doing and to stay current— you're playing with fire. It's just too easy to let it become a distraction.

The best antidote for jealousy or an inferiority complex (and we've all had them!) is to turn your attention back to bettering yourself. There is no sense at all in trying to copy someone else—you'll never be as good at what they do as they are. It's impossible. And likewise, no one will ever be as good at what you were born to do as you are. It is a waste to spend more than 10 percent of your time focusing on what others are doing. Spend most of your time focusing on how to improve your own unique gifts. It's realistically the only thing you can do anyway!

People envy what they're not doing themselves. When I was a kid and would watch other people's music videos, it was so easy to envy what they were doing because I wasn't doing it. I would watch Shakira and wish I was on a beach wearing a pretty dress. She looked really happy, and I wanted to be happy too.

Now, I'm the one on the beach with the pretty dress and wind in my hair. I don't envy others anymore because I'm actually living my dream. I'm doing it. And quite frankly, I don't have time to watch others and envy them anymore!

Now the focus has changed. There was a time St. Patrick's Day Irish dancing was not Diva Diverse's forte. It was something my team had to work on. Last year, I was a little worried when that day came around. We were booked for the entire day. It turned out we didn't get one complaint. But I wasn't satisfied with that. I still wanted to give people more. I wanted to give people the best show ever.

Spend your time working on yourself, and you won't have time to compare yourself to others.

Let's get real:
Have you been spending too much time comparing yourself to others?
What can you do about this now?

Collaborate; don't compete.

Another great way to crowd out envy from your life is to look for ways you can collaborate with other artists, rather than compete with them. If you're a singer/songwriter and you know of an artist you admire or aspire to be like, invite them to a songwriting session. Ask them if they'd like to perform at one of your shows. Put together a show with local talent you get inspiration from. If you meet someone who's great at what they do, and they would be an asset in your business, hire them. Ask them if they'd like to join the team. When you meet someone who impresses you, figure out how to work with them.

If you still find yourself getting competitive when you meet other talented artists in your craft, ask yourself, *Why would I want to compete with them when we could do something together?*

Let's get real:
Who in your craft have you been tempted to be jealous of? How can you collaborate with this artist instead?

Remember to be yourself.

It's important to learn how to adapt to any situation in business, but that doesn't mean you have to stop being yourself! You—your authentic self—are actually the most valuable asset in your company. You will have to do things for your fans, and you will have to take on various personas in the different roles as a business owner and entertainer, but underneath it all, stay true to who you are. Don't compromise your values or morals for anyone or anything.

I was listening to a JLo interview the other day. The interviewer said her new album had a lot of emotion, and she said the album was really her, in a personal way. They asked her what she meant and asked if her other albums weren't really her. She said some of her other albums were for her fans—she released music she knew they would want to hear. Sometimes you are going to have to wear a mask, but never change who you are underneath it, and don't forget to take it off frequently so you never forget who you are.

Let's get real:
How can you stay true to who you are, no matter which roles you need to move in and out of in your business?

FINAL THOUGHTS

Life is a circle. The end of one journey is the beginning of the next.
-JOSEPH M. MARSHALL III

Every night, Shane and I have a routine that includes a little meeting where we talk and catch up on the day and on things before we go to sleep. Life goes so fast, and sometimes those are the only moments we have together at the end of a busy day.

The other night, as we were lying in bed, he turned to me and said, "Hey, I was just wondering, when do you think your dance career's going to come to an end?"

I looked at him and I was like, "What?!"

He retracted. "No, no—I don't mean it like that." His voice got softer as he looked at me. "I actually genuinely want to know. I'm just curious to know, when do you think *you're* going to stop dancing? Not the company—the company will go on. But when will you feel like you've had enough?"

I paused. "You know what? I've actually really never thought of that. Maybe at forty? Maybe at fifty? Maybe at sixty? I mean, Cher's still prancing around on stage in costumes! And she's seventy-two! So I don't know!" I thought to myself for a few moments, and then turned back to Shane. "As long as people are booking me, and I'm healthy enough to be on stage, why would I stop? I think forever! Even if I'm acting, I'll still be acting to be a dancer in the film. I don't think I'll ever want to stop."

I had really never thought of it before. But I knew in that moment, more than I had ever known, that I was born a dancer, and I will die a dancer. It's who I was made to be.

People often say to me, "You're a business owner—what are you going to do for retirement?" It's the question I get asked most often at family dinners!

I always say, "Retirement? What do you mean? I *am* retired!" Even if I were sixty-five right now, I would be doing exactly what I'm already doing. I would never want to sit on a verandah swing and be bored or watch TV all day.

I'm very close to the seniors in my life. My great-grandmother just turned 101. She's walking, doesn't wear glasses, has no asthma, and doesn't take any pills. She might take an iron pill from time to time, but that's about it! And she's active. She's a member of a few groups and clubs. She goes out often. She has an itinerary every day. I am extremely inspired by her, and I don't see myself slowing down any time soon. As long as I'm healthy enough to dance, I'll be dancing.

Diva Diverse has been in business for eighteen years. The eighteen-year anniversary was February 20th, 2003. I'm not a hoarder, but I'm very sentimental with my stuff. I have a book that all my past dancers wrote in one year. They wrote wonderful things about me in this book, things that were true for them in the moment. They said that I had taught them so much and that they loved me. They said they appreciated the company.

Most of them are not with me today. The rest of them have either gone to school, gotten married, moved out of the country, or left and opened their own companies. I was looking at it the other day and thinking some people might be tempted to throw it away because a lot of the people who wrote in it caused me pain years later. But they also caused me growth, and I forgive them. It's actually amazing to look back on. Some really beautiful moments were captured in that book.

It's been an amazing journey, and I am grateful for every single moment. Everything has become a blessing.

As I finish the editing for this book, it's September 8, 2020, and we are slowly recovering from the Covid-19 pandemic. It's been a really rough year for everyone. Somehow, I've managed to steer the company in a new direction.

Falesha Homes was born in 2017; that's when I officially became a realtor. I had a vision for this company to be the Diva Diverse of the real estate industry. Due to the lockdown in March, I've been able to put 110 percent into the growth of the business. The team and I are currently buying, selling, renovating, staging, and building homes for our clients. I'm really excited for the latest venture in my life, but mostly looking forward to having you join me on this journey.

I am so grateful to have been able to share my life with you. Thank you for your generosity in spending this time with me. In reading this book, you have started a journey of writing and expressing your desires, hopes, dreams, fears, and reflections. Don't stop now. You've just begun, and there is so much more about yourself and your business to discover. I invite you to continue to apply everything you saw for yourself in this book to your life.

May you always follow DIVA in the direction of becoming the fullest expression of who you have always been, and will always be.

REFERENCES

Maxwell, John C. *Beyond Talent: Become Someone Who Gets Extraordinary Results*. New York: Thomas Nelson Inc, 2011, p. 10.

Markham, Edwin, 21st Century American Poet.

Westlake, Courtney. "Why Letting Others Help You Is a Gift." https://www.courtneywestlake.com/why-letting-others-help-you-is-a-gift/

ABOUT THE AUTHOR

A serial entrepreneur and entertainer, Falesha Raquel is in the business of developing the creativity, passion, drive, and business intelligence of everyone in her community. Falesha's dance career stemmed from an opportunity to perform for her aunt and uncle on their wedding day at the early age of seven. From that moment forward, she knew she had to find a way to continue performing. Everything was aligning, and Falesha just knew she found her purpose. She started her talent agency, Diva Diverse, when she was fifteen years old in Toronto, Canada, with a mission to give dancers an opportunity to develop their skills and perform as much as possible, despite their cultural backgrounds, size, or dance experience. Falesha was eager to train dancers who had the three things important to her: passion, loyalty, and commitment. With a love for dance and a desire for growth, she expanded her company and decided to bring it south to Miami in 2014. Diva Diverse offers their clients a wide range of productions and continues to entertain audiences across North America.

After fifteen years of successfully running Diva Diverse, Falesha wanted to explore her passion in real estate. Her father-in-law had been a builder for more than fifty years. Being around construction all the time and real estate really sparked her interest. In 2017 she got her real estate license and had the opportunity to partner with some of the city's well-known developers who mentored and guided her. She founded Falesha Homes Inc. and now serves clients within Ontario who are buying, selling, renovating, or building their dream home from scratch.

All through Falesha's life, she was always called a diva. She loved weekly shopping, makeup, and the finer things in life. She always struggled to find the perfect match when it came to makeup due to her mixed ethnicity and usually felt like a lot of products were overpriced. When she was younger, she had a goal that one day she would have her own makeup line. She finally made that come to reality on March 6, 2019, and FR BEAUTY was born.

Falesha has a philosophy: If you are not growing, you are not living. She will continue to grow and do new things; it's just her personality and who she is, and she encourages her community to embrace growth and try new things.

Stayed tuned as Falesha Raquel will be launching some new exciting projects, partnerships, and plans in 2021 to help you find inspiration and live your best life.

www.falesharaquel.com
Info@falesha.com
647-888-7772

ENDNOTES

1   Maxwell, John C. *Beyond Talent: Become Someone Who Gets Extraordinary Results.* p.10, New York: Thomas Nelson Inc, 2011.

2   Markham, Edwin, Twenty-first Century American Poet.

3   Westlake, Courtney. "Why Letting Others Help You Is a Gift." https://www.courtneywestlake.com/why-letting-others-help-you-is-a-gift/

www.ingramcontent.com/pod-product-compliance
Lightning Source LLC
Chambersburg PA
CBHW051653060726
47593CB00021B/636